CURIOSITIES OF THE

CONFEDERATE CAPITAL

UNTOLD RICHMOND STORIES OF THE

SPECTACULAR
TRAGIC
AND
BIZARRE

BRIAN BURNS

Charleston · London

THE
History
PRESS

Published by The History Press
Charleston, SC 29403
www.historypress.net

Copyright © 2013 by Brian Burns
All rights reserved

Front cover, cavalry image: Appears in Richard Wheeler's *Sword Over Richmond.* New York:
Harper and Row, 1986.

First published 2013

Manufactured in the United States

ISBN 978.1.60949.954.9

Library of Congress CIP data applied for.

For Judd Proctor,
the tireless freedom fighter

For Trudy Bryan —
Great to meet you!

[signature]

CONTENTS

Introduction   7

1. Disaster on Brown's Island
   Explosion Devastates Female Workforce   9
2. Police Raid at Midnight
   Mayor Mayo Declares War on Gambling Saloons   13
3. Eye in the Sky
   The Confederate Balloon Gazelle   18
4. "The Lion"
   James Lyons, Fire-Eater and Master of "Laburnum"   22
5. Bloody Caravan from Seven Pines
   Richmond Becomes One Vast Hospital   35
6. Violet's War
   Tragedy and Mayhem in the Countryside   44
7. Cheers at the Richmond Theatre
   Culture Amid the Chaos   47
8. Camp Lee
   Richmond's Chief Camp of Instruction   54
9. The Mordecai Ladies
   Emotions Run High at "Rosewood"   65

Contents

10. Coping Without Coffee
   Coffee Substitute Factory Meets Violent End   76
11. Born Fighter, Mary Edwards Walker
   Union Doctor Imprisoned at the Castle   79
12. Moonlight Counterfeiters
   Facing the Wrath of the Confederate Court   84
13. The Brook Church Fight
   Forgotten Battle Claims Colonel James Byron Gordon   87
14. Foreign Assistance
   French Novel Eases Confederate Miseries   92
15. Richmond's Queen of Hospitality
   The Making of the City's Virtual Salon   94
16. The Dreaded Whipping Post
   Punishment Ordered in Mayor Mayo's Court   102
17. Fanfare at Rocketts Wharf
   Arrival of Confederate Prisoners of War   106
18. Beckman's Saloon Down on Main
   A Snapshot of the City's Underbelly   109
19. George Arents and the Lincoln Conspiracy
   Rumors Fly About Local Merchant   111
20. Avenging the "Traitoress"
   Rush to Judgment for Mary Caroline Allan   115
21. Miracle in the Trenches
   Hungry Soldiers Offered a Bountiful Spread   123
22. Chester's Campaign
   Black War Correspondent Trumpets the End of Slavery   125

Notes   135
Bibliography   145
Index   157
About the Author   159

INTRODUCTION

When Richmond was chosen as the Capital of the Confederacy, it was a recipe for unimaginable dramas on the city's home front—some exhilarating, some devastating and some downright odd. The vast majority of those dramas have never been uncovered.

To find the freshest stories, I simply followed my nose. Several times I found a fascinating blurb and discovered that no one had ever pieced together the entire story. In other cases, I discovered that important people or places had practically been forgotten. I also came across some unusual news items in Richmond's Civil War newspapers and wanted to share them in a unique way.

Modern technology was a huge help. Many of those newspapers have been transcribed online, and I could search by keyword to track developing stories. This opened up a wealth of information and local color. Combined with other credible sources in print and online, including the *Southern Historical Society Papers*, a crisp picture of Richmond's city life comes into view. We can almost imagine what it was like to live there during the bloodiest war in our nation's history. The hunger brought on by food shortages. The roller coaster of emotions. A wild proliferation of gambling and prostitution. A penal code that seems straight out of the dark ages. A war hospital on every corner, marked by the smell of death. And, perhaps most dramatically, the nearly constant threat of enemy invasion and conquest.

Obviously, the war impacted everyone differently, depending on his or her station in life. A war-torn soldier lying on a hospital cot had a far different perspective than the queen of fashionable society. A slave's experience had practically nothing in common with that of a wealthy auctioneer of blockade goods. And there was no comparison between the daily lives of a Confederate congressman and an impoverished, nine-year-old girl working in a gun cartridge factory.

This book isn't intended to chronicle every event or the entire cast of characters in the city from 1861 to 1865. But it bears witness to the super-tumultuous state of affairs and fills in gaps in the history. Some stories may surprise you. Some may make you cringe. And some may make you laugh.

I hope this collection gives you an understanding of the war—and Richmond—that you didn't have before.

Chapter 1

DISASTER ON BROWN'S ISLAND

Explosion Devastates Female Workforce

The explosion on Brown's Island in May 1863 sent a long, thunderous roar through the streets of Richmond. Hundreds of town folk scurried toward the plume of dense smoke to see what happened. It was Friday the thirteenth.

About two years earlier, the brush on the island was cleared, and low, frame buildings were constructed for the manufacture of gun cartridges and the like. The factory was termed the Confederate States Laboratory. Cranking out nearly 1,200 cartridges a day, it had recently been called "the salvation of the Confederacy." But now the workers were the ones in need of salvation. And most of them were white women and girls—just nine to twenty years old—desperately trying to provide for their needy families.

One of the buildings, where eighty to one hundred of the females were working, was "blown into a complete wreck, the roof lifted off, and the walls dashed out, the ruins falling upon the operatives."[1]

Eighteen-year-old Mary Ryan had been loading explosive powder into friction primers—the highly explosive devices used to ignite gunpowder in cannons and other field pieces. At one end of the room was a coal-burning stove. Mary's friction primer got stuck in a "varnishing board," so she slammed the board three times on the table to drive the primer out. In a flash, she was thrown to the ceiling, and the whole place erupted in flames. About ten females were killed instantly, and many others were burned beyond recognition. The *Richmond Enquirer* painted a vivid picture of the carnage: "Some had an arm or a leg divested of flesh and skin, others were bleeding with wounds received from the falling timbers or in the violent concussions against floor and ceiling which ensued."[2] A few females, with their clothes on fire, plunged into the river.

As men quickly dowsed the burning wreckage, doctors rushed in from nearby General Hospital No. 2—a tobacco factory turned war hospital. When they reached the accident site, "the most heart rending lamentations and cries" were heard amongst the ruins "from sufferers rendered delirious from suffering and terror."[3] The doctors didn't waste a second. They removed the victims' clothing and covered their bodies thickly with flour and cotton, saturated with oil. They also administered chloroform.

Meanwhile, loved ones ran onto the scene. "Mothers rushed about, throwing themselves upon the corpses of the dead and the persons of the wounded," the *Examiner* reported.[4] Doctors quickly loaded the victims into carriages and farm wagons and dispatched them toward General Hospital No. 2, just four blocks north at Cary and Seventh Streets. As the horse-drawn vehicles reached the city side of the bridge, citizens crowded along the canal bank began to grasp the scope of the tragedy. Even though they were accustomed to seeing hundreds of bloodied soldiers arrive in the city for care, they were horrified. These victims were their friends and neighbors.

General Hospital No. 2 didn't remotely resemble a modern-day burn unit, so the worst cases didn't stand a chance. The day following the tragedy, the death toll climbed to twenty-nine. The day after that, Mary Ryan died at her father's house in Oregon Hill, and several victims' funeral processions crisscrossed the city.

Already rallying to one cause, Richmond rallied to another. Mayor Mayo asked the YMCA to help raise a relief fund for the victims and their families. A committee was appointed to solicit donations, and employees of the Richmond Arsenal and Laboratory pitched in. Two performing arts theaters in the city also donated the proceeds of a night's entertainment to the effort.

Men serving on the battlefield were touched. When hearing of the mayor's appeal to Richmonders, one soldier wrote to the *Richmond Sentinel*, "A non-resident of the city, I beg to appeal to all humane people in the city and the State, to contribute to so laudable a purpose. The poor wounded creatures are young females who were dependent on their daily labor for their support. I send you five dollars and am only sorry I cannot afford more."[5]

Nearly a month after the accident, a girl's body was pulled from the James River. She was one of the explosion victims reported missing.

In the end, at least forty-five people died as a result of the explosion. A few of them were males, including sixty-three-year-old laboratory official Reverend John Woodcock, and a fifteen-year-old boy. But most of the dead were young girls caught up in a war they were incapable of understanding.

———◆———

When the war was over, tourists came in droves from all over to see the legendary Capital of the Confederacy. In the summer of 1865, Northern novelist John Townsend Trowbridge traveled to Richmond to document the war prisons, training camps, battlefields and former slave auction houses. On his visit to Belle Isle, where Union prisoners of war had been held by the thousands, he crossed paths with a dirtied laborer headed home from the nail factory there. After brief introductions, the laborer offered Trowbridge a ride to the city in a skiff. Trowbridge began pressing the laborer for details about wartime goings-on in the city.

As the men drifted close to an islet, the laborer opened up. "This yer is Brown's Island," he said. "You've heerd of the laboratory, whar they made ammunition fo' the army?" He pointed out the deserted buildings and began recounting the 1863 explosion. As the pair reached the city side of the Brown's Island bridge, another man offered to pick up the rest of the story. Old, haggard and filthy, he seemed half-crazed. "My daughter was work'n' thar at the time; and she was blowed all to pieces! All to pieces! My God, my God, it was horrible!" the old man exclaimed. "Come to my house, and you shall see her; if you don't believe me, you shall see her! Blowed all to pieces, all to pieces, my God!"

Trowbridge wasn't sure what to expect. When they arrived at the house, the girl was standing at the front door, very much alive. Horrible scars covered her face and hands.

"Look!" the man said. "All to pieces, as I told you!"

"Don't, don't, pa!" the girl begged. Turning to Trowbridge, she whispered, "You mustn't mind him. He is a little out of his head."

"He has been telling me how you were blown up in the laboratory," Trowbridge said sympathetically. "You must have suffered fearfully from those wounds!"

"Oh yes, there was five weeks nobody thought I would live," the girl replied. "But I didn't mind it," she added with a smile, "for it was in a good cause."

Most Southerners would have applauded the girl's blind devotion. But as Trowbridge later wrote, in unvarnished nineteenth-century sexism, "...she was not insane; she was a woman. A man may be reasoned and beaten out of a false opinion, but a woman never. She will not yield to logic, not even to the logic of events."

Today, Brown's Island is a peaceful retreat, and the explosion of 1863 is merely a memory. There is an occasional blast there, however, during the annual Richmond Folk Festival.

Chapter 2

POLICE RAID AT MIDNIGHT

Mayor Mayo Declares War on Gambling Saloons

After Richmond was named the Confederate Capital and flooded with opportunists and black marketeers, it became a seething cauldron of crime and vice. In fact, many citizens complained that robbers and gamblers had taken possession of the city. Forty gambling saloons were clustered near the Exchange Hotel at Fourteenth and Franklin Streets, where men were hot for faro—a card game in which players bet on a special board as the dealer drew two cards from his box. These so-called "faro banks" were big business. In fact, there were so many of them that a Southern wit re-christened the city, "Farobankopolis."

Oddly enough, these saloons were packed with leading men of the city—wealthy merchants, slave traders, Confederate officers and government officials. Some were army quartermasters and commissaries who gambled away the public funds. And some were "fraudulent officers whose title of 'Colonel' had been bestowed in the brothels."[6]

The faro banks were enticing, with their "luxurious furniture, soft lights, obsequious servants and lavish store of such wines and liquors and cigars as could be had nowhere else in Dixie."[7] They were a careful, urbane blending of speakeasy and men's club. Complimentary, sumptuous suppers were spread before the patrons at 11:00 p.m. For some, the scene was a welcome escape from dreary camp life:

> Senators, soldiers and the learned professions sat elbow to elbow, round
> the generous table that offered choicest viands money could procure. In the

handsome rooms above they puffed fragrant and real Havanas, while the latest developments of news, strategy and policy were discussed; sometimes ably, sometimes flippantly, but always freshly. Here men who had been riding raids in the mountains of the West; had lain shut up in the water batteries of the Mississippi; or had faced the advance of the many "On-to-Richmonds"—met after long separation. Here the wondering young cadet would look first upon some noted raider, or some gallant brigadier—cool and invincible amid the rattle of Minié-balls, as reckless but conquerable amid the rattle of ivory chips.[8]

No matter who bellied up to a faro table, the stakes were high. At one sitting, a player could win $500 or lose anywhere from $1,000 to $5,000. Reportedly, a few lost as much as $20,000 in a single night.[9]

Because the faro banks operated outside the law, there was often "a huge buck negro at the front door to keep watch," said the *Whig.*[10]

In the fall of 1861, Mayor Joseph Mayo planned a surprise attack on the faro banks. On Saturday, November 9—at the stroke of midnight—ax-wielding police simultaneously raided several establishments, making arrests and confiscating property.

Joseph Mayo, wartime mayor. His midnight raid on the gambling houses "occasioned nearly as much sensation as the great battle of Manassas." *Library of Virginia.*

One of the gambling houses targeted in the raid—on Fourteenth Street between Main and Franklin—was operated by thirty-three-year-old Johnny Worsham. Johnny's place—"where the wine was excellent, the furniture regal, and the play high"—was the "favorite gambling resort of Confederate dignitaries."[11] It had a stage for dancing girls. By the door stood "two giant black bouncers in bowler hats and identical suits."[12] The most notorious gambler frequenting the house was Judah P. Benjamin, who climbed the political ladder from attorney general to secretary of war, and finally to secretary of state.

When two officers stormed Johnny's place on this November night, they found faro tables, roulette tables and cards. Men were standing around like deer in the headlights.[13] The officers ransacked the place for cash, even rifling through Johnny's pockets, and confiscated $543. Johnny was arrested without incident and slapped with "keeping and exhibiting the game of faro," a misdemeanor charge. Police hauled away some of Johnny's property, in a "grand and imposing" procession to the station house. The *Dispatch* furnished a vivid picture:

Judah P. Benjamin, high-ranking Confederate official and faro lover. He escaped police raids due to his "dexterity in leaping from the back doors of the gambling-hells." *Drum-Beat of the Nation.*

It was indeed a sight to see our sturdy officers, during the small hours of Sunday morning, moving silently along under the weight of the massive legs of a faro table, while their companions toted the other component parts; for the apparatus was knocked to pieces to facilitate transportation. There were roulette tables, faro tables and drawers, and silver dealing boxes, all of the most approved style and exquisite workmanship; then there was something like half a bushel of ivory checks, or "chips," which represent money in these popular houses, ranging in denomination from 25 cents to $100; besides cues, playing cards, layouts, and all the paraphernalia of great and little gambling establishments.[14]

If Johnny was proven guilty in court, the police were authorized to burn every bit of the haul. The editor of the *Dispatch* considered this horribly wasteful, since there were shortages of even basic commodities. "It seems almost like wickedness to destroy [the faro table] in such times as these," the paper argued, adding, "Articles that have served a bad purpose might be made to serve a good one."[15]

Johnny turned the tables on the police and charged them with trespassing. He sued for $5,000 in damages but quickly lost that fight.[16]

On December 13, about a month after he was arrested, Johnny was arraigned at city hall near Capital Square. On his defense team was William W. Crump, soon to be assistant secretary of the Confederate Treasury. Johnny pleaded not guilty and was released on $3,000 bail. Within hours, his trial was already underway. Called as witnesses were the policemen involved in the raid. Then, in a dramatic move, the prosecutor presented Exhibit A—two elaborately finished faro tables.[17]

After just a few days, the case went to the jury. There were eight votes for acquittal and four for conviction. Johnny was granted a new trial.[18] Also bogged down in the courts were the other gambling saloons involved in the November raid.

Clearly, the mayor was fighting a losing battle. His police force was no match for Richmond's crime epidemic, and the city had a virtual army of top-rate defense attorneys. In fact, attorneys were said to be the only ones benefiting from the raid. The crackdown was considered an utter failure. "The moral atmosphere still reeks with the taint of "gambling hells," said the *Dispatch* on December 16. "We think the gamblers hold all the trumps and all the honors, and the municipal authorities might as well give up the game."[19] Soon, however, the Virginia legislature would make a play of its own.

Two days after Christmas, at high noon, a huge bonfire raged in front of city hall on Broad Street. A curious crowd gathered. Going up in smoke was the faro equipment from the November raid. All but Johnny's, that is. His case was still pending.

But in early 1862, Johnny finally lost.

The next year, on October 16, 1863, the Virginia legislature passed a much stiffer gaming law. Those convicted for "keeping or exhibiting" a gaming table known as a "faro bank" faced a jail term of two to twelve months and a fine of $100 to $1,000. And, at the discretion of the court, guilty parties could be whipped on the bare back, not to exceed thirty-nine "stripes."

Armed with the new law, Mayor Mayo didn't waste any time in going after Johnny's fashionable gambling palace again. Just three days after the new law went into effect, the police got a warrant to enter his establishment in Corinthian Hall on Main Street, in the shadow of the Confederate Treasury. A party was found playing bluff, using ivory chips as counters. Johnny and six servants were arrested and taken into custody, and his furniture was again hauled to the station house.[20]

In a matter of days, however, Johnny was a free man and his furniture was returned to him. It should have come as no surprise. The police simply hadn't found any money boxes or other faro-bank paraphernalia in the establishment.[21] Johnny resumed his business for nearly a decade, keeping one step ahead of the law.

Although Johnny Worsham was a native Richmonder, he never served in the Confederate army. He paid $1,200 for a substitute. In a sense, the Yankees helped him foot the bill, as he owned another fashionable faro-bank on Broadway in New York City.[22]

Chapter 3

EYE IN THE SKY

The Confederate Balloon *Gazelle*

Crowds flocked to Philadelphia on September 8, 1860, and snapped up their fifty-cent tickets for a spectacular exhibition. Amidst a carnival-like atmosphere, showman Professor Thaddeus Sobieski Coulincourt Lowe was about to launch his mammoth balloon, *The Great Western.* The Northern scientific genius announced he was going to cross the Atlantic Ocean by balloon—a feat never before attempted. He inflated his balloon at the Philadelphia Gas Works. But a half hour before the scheduled departure, the balloon was ripped open by a stiff wind.[23]

Like Albert Einstein, Thomas Edison or any great inventor, Lowe didn't give up. With another balloon, the *Enterprise,* he planned a test flight for April 20, 1861—just days after the surrender of Fort Sumter in South Carolina. Taking off from Cincinnati, he intended to fly to Washington, D.C. By sheer coincidence, the winds landed him in war-crazed South Carolina, where he was accused of being "an inhabitant of some ethereal or infernal region"—the devil himself.

When soldiers North and South began their big face-off, Lowe ditched his transatlantic dreams and looked to gathering intelligence on the Confederates for the Union army. Newspapers in the North began harping on the value of Union balloons. Richmond papers scoffed at the suggestion. "They propose balloons to go up and inspect our camps, and drop missiles upon our soldiers," the *Richmond Dispatch* tittered. "They are as likely to hit the mark in that way as any other, and we hope they will try it. If they descend low enough to form a target as big as a snow-ball, one of our riflemen will take the gas out of their balloon and the aeronaut with a single shot."[24] Before long, the *Dispatch* editor would have to eat a huge hunk of humble pie.

In June 1861, Lowe met with President Lincoln and laid out his ideas for balloon reconnaissance. He suggested sending telegrams from the balloon to the commanders below and even offered the president a live demonstration. The *Dispatch* reported on the event. "Professor Lowe experimented with his army balloon this afternoon from the Columbia Armory grounds," the paper began. "He made a number of ascensions, taking up with him a telegraphing apparatus, to which was attached a wire connecting with the President's house. He sent from his aerial perch a dispatch to the President and received a reply from him."[25]

Lowe's message read:

> *Balloon "Enterprise," Washington, June 17, 1861*
> *To the President of the United States*
>
> *Sir:*
> *This point of observation commands an area nearly fifty miles in diameter. The city, with its girdle of encampments, presents a superb scene. I take great pleasure in sending you this first dispatch ever telegraphed from an aerial station, and in acknowledging my indebtedness to your encouragement for the opportunity of demonstrating the availability of the science of aeronautics in the military service of this country.*
>
> > *Yours respectfully,*
> > *T.S.C. Lowe*

For the rest of the evening, the *Enterprise* was moored on the south lawn of the White House, where Lowe was an honored guest. Still, the *Dispatch* editor believed the balloonist clung to his showman ways, calling him a "humbug" intent on "bamboozling" the Lincoln administration to "pocket a few thousand."[26]

Since most white Richmonders detested President Lincoln for leading an assault on the South and threatening slavery, local papers took a long line of jabs at him. "A tale is told in Washington that Old Abe went up with Professor Lowe in his famous balloon one day last week, to reconnoitre the position of the 'rebel' forces," said a letter in the *Dispatch* on July 12. "They had not proceeded very high before Old Abe, tapping his companion on the shoulder, cried out, 'Hold, Professor, I think I see a masked battery just below us here. Don't you think we had better return?'"[27] The paper was all too eager to paint Lincoln as a wimp.

By the next month, Lincoln was sold on Lowe's balloons for the Union war effort. The president established a balloon corps under Lowe's command to provide aerial reconnaissance for Northern armies, as well as to provide aerial telegraphy services. Heralded as "King of the Clouds," Lowe quickly proved his chops in the war. On September 24, 1861, he ascended to more than one thousand feet near Arlington, Virginia, and began telegraphing intelligence on the Confederate troops located at Falls Church, Virginia. Union guns were aimed and fired accurately at the Confederate troops without actually being able to see them—a first in the history of warfare.

As Lowe secretly enlarged his fleet, Union balloons were causing many a Confederate headache. General Longstreet said, "We watched with envious eyes their beautiful observations as they floated high up in the air, well out of range of our guns."

Finally, Confederates swallowed their pride and decided to try "the enemy's plan of playing bird's-eye bo-peep."[28] But there was a problem—balloon silk couldn't be imported because of the Union blockade of ports. So, experienced balloon builder and aeronaut Charles Cevor made a balloon in Savannah from bolts of colored silk intended for ladies' dresses. (The widely circulated story that the balloon was made from silk dresses donated by Confederate ladies is sweet, but pure mythological bunk.)

When the *Gazelle* was completed, the Confederates were engaged in a bitter fight with Union forces on the peninsula, and Richmond was under serious threat. The balloon was arduously transported five hundred miles, arriving in the city on June 24. There it was filled with illumination gas at the city gas works—just in time for the bloody Seven Days' battles.

Because the *Gazelle* leaked and needed to be refilled frequently, the Confederates devised a way to transport it back and forth from the Virginia Peninsula. It was tethered to a boxcar on land and run down the York River Railroad. Then, on June 27, a quick study named Lieutenant Colonel Edward Porter Alexander took the *Gazelle* up about two miles outside Richmond on the Williamsburg Road (in the vicinity of today's Montrose Elementary School). But unlike Union balloonists, he didn't have telegraph equipment. He used a signaling system he'd developed, using "four big, black-cambric balls," suspended underneath the balloon's control basket. Meanwhile, the Union had two larger balloons gathering reconnaissance just four miles away. History was made again. It was the first time that opposing

The Battle of Seven Pines, with reconnaissance balloon in background. *Library of Congress.*

"air forces" faced each other in warfare. The *Gazelle*—as small, homely and leaky as it was—helped convince Union General McClellan to retreat from the outskirts of Richmond.

But just days later, the career of the *Gazelle* ended. On July 4, the deflated balloon was packed aboard the CSS *Teaser*, an armed tugboat that had run aground in the James River near Berkeley Plantation. Two Federal warships, the *Monitor* and the *Maratanza*, drifted onto the scene, dwarfing the tug. The *Maratanza* blasted the *Teaser* with canister shot, and the Confederates abandoned ship. The next shot hit its boiler and exploded.

When the Federals boarded the wreckage to inspect their prize, they found not only the balloon but also several mines—and documents detailing where they were to be placed in the river. Longstreet called the capture "the meanest trick of the war."

Not long after the Seven Days' Battles, the remnants of the *Gazelle* were presented to Professor Lowe in Washington. He described it as "a veritable Joseph's coat of many colors," explaining that "the fashions in silks at that period were ornate, large flowery patterns, squares and plaids in blues, greens, crimsons, ebony and rich heavy watered silks."

Later, the balloon was cut into pieces and given to various members of Congress and others as mementos. Lowe kept one of the larger pieces himself.

Chapter 4

"The Lion"

James Lyons, Fire-Eater and Master of "Laburnum"

S pirits of the Revolution!" implored prominent Richmond lawyer, James Lyons, in 1856. "Arouse the sleeping energies of your sons, and lead them to resistance, to victory and to independence!"

He was speaking in Savannah at the Southern Commercial Convention, which had shifted its focus from the Southern economy to politics. Lyons warned the Southerners to prepare for the worst. Northern antagonism toward slavery was escalating, and the antislavery Republicans could possibly take the White House that November. In that event, Lyons urged the Southern States to proclaim their independence and "prepare for the conflict, if conflict must come." With his usual eloquence, he argued, "This Union has been glorious, and is dear to the heart of every patriot; but liberty, honor, independence are dearer far."[29]

As fate would have it, the crisis blew over until four years later, when Abraham Lincoln got elected in 1860. James Lyons, then fifty-nine years old, got right back on his soapbox. An intrepid civic leader and slaveholder, he called African slavery "a blessing." He also asserted that the ungentlemanly "rail-splitter" had gotten elected because of his "avowal of his enmity" to the South and its "rights and institutions."

Lyons had served twice in the Virginia State Senate and once in the House. After South Carolina seceded that December, "the Lion" roared louder than ever—declaring that the "abolition government" was intent on "southern ruin." In early 1861—with Virginia still heavily Unionist—he urged the

State to secede before Lincoln's army "marches upon you, to slaughter your people and desolate your land." To spread his gospel, Lyons published a rambling treatise in the *Richmond Enquirer* under the pen name "Virginius." He believed the South shouldn't listen to those who advised waiting for an overt act by the North. "Would they commit the lamb to the wolf, in the hope that his nature and appetite would change before he devoured it?" he reasoned.

At the heart of Lyons's diatribe was that "the southern states should, without delay," form a new confederacy, "in which their people will be safe from the aggressions of their enemies, and may enjoy their property, in peace, surrounded by plenty." By "property," he meant *slaves*—and he insisted "the constitution acknowledges and guarantees our property in them."

Aristocratic fire-eater James Lyons, one of Richmond's earliest voices for secession. *The Museum of the Confederacy, Richmond, Virginia.*

There was no saving the so-called "glorious Union" anyway, Lyons claimed, because there was no glory left. "For years," he said, the Union's glory "has been acquired by the violation of the constitution, and the pillage and oppression of the south."[30]

A polished Virginia aristocrat married to the young, beautiful and moneyed Imogen Penn, Lyons had a lot at stake. He owned dozens of slaves and a picturesque, 160-acre plantation in Henrico County called "Laburnum." It was situated about a mile and a half north of Richmond on Brook Turnpike—today's Brook Road. There, on the site of an old frame roadhouse called the Paradise Inn, Lyons in the late 1850s created his own paradise—a stately plantation home. With its broad veranda, tall white columns and a wide expanse of lawn, it could have doubled for "Tara" from *Gone with the Wind*. The mansion was described as "a typical home of the gentry, having the English exclusiveness in delightful amalgam with genuine American hospitality."[31] Stretching beyond the lawn were stables, orchards and fields of wheat and corn. Soon, Laburnum's gracious parlors would crackle with war intrigue.

Lyons was certainly pleased on February 8, 1861, when six states created the Confederate States of America in Montgomery, Alabama—and positively exultant when Virginia seceded that April. In fact, as the Secession Convention was in its final hours of deliberation on April 16, Lyons joined in a radical tirade at the so-called People's Convention at Metropolitan Hall. With a voice "loud and strong" and a face "frank and manly," he had a commanding presence.[32] Other fire-eating secessionists in the hall included George Wythe Randolph, Thomas Jefferson's grandson; and O. Jennings Wise, son of a former Virginia governor and chief editor of the *Richmond Enquirer*.

Just days after Virginia formally seceded by popular vote that May, the Confederate Congress decided to move the capital of the Confederacy to Lyons's hometown. Then, that June, war arrived on Virginia's doorstep.

Lyons quickly put his legal talents to work for the Confederacy. He served as a trial judge of political prisoners, a few of them suspected of being spies. Lyons recommended release for some and upheld imprisonment for others. He judged some as traitors "that ought to be hung."[33]

Like most wealthy Richmond gentlemen too old for field service, Lyons pitched in however he could to help the cause. In July 1861, right after the bloodbath at Manassas, he was part of a committee "for the reception and accommodation of sick and wounded soldiers from the scene of war." The committee solicited "contributions of chickens, eggs, fresh butter, sage, and other articles, which may contribute to the comfort of our disabled men."[34]

Lyons didn't know it yet, but he would soon trade butter-and-egg collecting for a high post in the Confederate government. On January 18, 1862, Confederate congressman John Tyler—a former president of the United States—died in Richmond while staying at the Exchange Hotel. Four days later, a group of gentlemen formally requested that James Lyons announce himself a candidate to fill the vacancy. He graciously accepted.[35] The *Dispatch* endorsed Lyons, saying he was "one of the most faithful and vigilant sentinels on the watch-tower of the South." He was also "thoroughly versed in parliamentary usage," the paper added, "while his mind is both strong and quick in its action, always prepared to grasp the knotty points of a debate, and prompt to apply the rule and solve them."[36] Even the *Richmond Enquirer* endorsed Lyons, because he advocated secession "when to avow [its] principles found more frowns than smiles."[37] In the February 10 election, Lyons won.

But within a month of taking his seat, Lyons was tempted to resign. He considered his fellow congressmen unfit for the task and was irked by displays of "jealousy, selfish ambition and consequent discord." His wife convinced him to remain, since his resignation could be misread as disaffection with the cause. Lyons quickly proved himself "a pillar of the administration" and one of President Davis's closest friends and allies. At the president's second

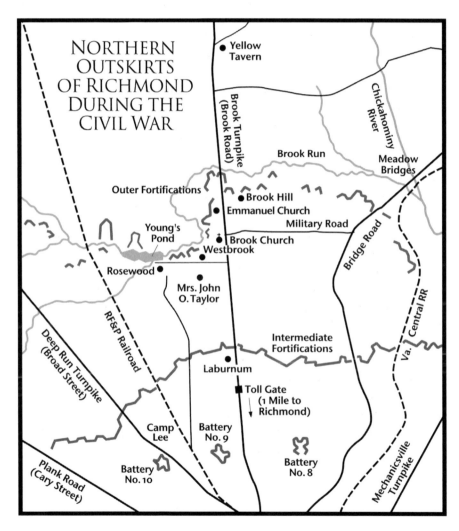

Map created by author. Sources: Map of the defenses of Richmond & Petersburg, from the Official Records Atlas, Plate C, #2. Prepared by Nathaniel Micheler, 1865; Vicinity of Richmond map, from the Official Records Atlas, Plate XCII, #1. Prepared by Captain A.H. Campbell (CSA).

inauguration on February 22, 1862, in a torrential downpour on the capitol grounds, Lyons called the massive assemblage to order.[38]

James Lyons's beautiful wife, Imogen, was from a wealthy New Orleans family, whose cash helped subsidize the lavish lifestyle at Laburnum. The mansion was nicknamed "the Lyons' den" for Imogen's occasional yet spirited indulgences in "chronique scandaleuse"—first-rate Richmond gossip. Otherwise, Imogen was a positively charming hostess. Throughout the war years, she and her husband elegantly entertained the cream of war society. Among their guests were President Jefferson Davis and his wife, Varina; members of Davis's cabinet; English and French nobility; and many top generals, including Robert E. Lee. They all basked in the Lyonses' rich appointments, including "furniture imported from Europe, massive silver, shelves lined with books, elaborate carriages, thoroughbred horses, and legions of servants." Varina Davis thought "a finer example of a high-bred Virginia household could not have been found."[39] President Davis often rode out to Laburnum to visit the city's intermediate fortifications on the farm and took tea with the Lyonses.

On three occasions, James Lyons was required to send a male slave to labor on the city's fortifications. With more slaves than most whites, he had once quoted with approval the English philosopher Edmund Burke: "Slaves are often much attached to their masters…It is sometimes as hard to persuade slaves to be free as it is to compel free men to be slaves." It may have come as a surprise to Lyons, then, when several of his slaves ran away during the war. Typically, Lyons placed an ad in the *Dispatch* offering a reward for their return. In one, he offered a $300 reward "for the apprehension of my boy Billy," a seventeen-year-old "good cook." He described him as "a mulatto of delicate frame and slightly aquiline face."[40]

Billy's older brother, John Mitchell, was more loyal. He and his wife, Rebecca, lived at Laburnum. In July 1863, they had a son, John Mitchell Jr., who would grow up to become the fearless editor of the *Richmond Planet*. In that role, he'd expose "racial injustice wherever it lurked," such as lynchings, segregation and the rise of the Ku Klux Klan.

In the spring of 1862, the French government considered formally extending an offer for mediation of the war. With his "courtly manners," Lyons opened his Laburnum mansion to Count Mercier, the French minister. As Lyons put it, Mercier was visiting Richmond "by permission of the Northern Government, but was interdicted from holding direct intercourse with President Davis or any of his Cabinet." Mercier had been sent by Lincoln's secretary of state, William H. Seward, as a peacemaker. After Lyons welcomed the French minister to Laburnum—followed, no doubt, by white-gloved servants serving refreshments from silver trays—the two men got down to business in the library. "Can't this war be stopped?" Mercier asked. "Can't you come back under the old flag?"

"I suppose that is impossible," Lyons replied, "for Mr. Seward would not permit us to do so without the abolition of slavery, and it would be useless to propose that to the men from the extreme South."

"You are mistaken," Mercier insisted. "If you will only return and acknowledge the flag, Mr. Seward will permit you to return without any conditions."

"What!" Lyons said, "*with* the institution of slavery?"

"Yes," Mercier declared.

Lyons had one remaining concern. "We cannot live hereafter in the state of harassment and excitement in which we have lived for some years past," he asserted.

Mercier pointed to a piece of paper on the table and said, "Mr. Seward will allow you to write your own guarantees."

The plot thickened a few months later, when Lyons tried to broker a deal at Laburnum with the French consul, Monsieur Paul. They discussed the French emperor's possible acknowledgment of the Confederate government. Monsieur Paul suggested passing "some bill for the gradual abolition of slavery in fifty or sixty years." The next morning, before Congress met, Lyons went to see President Davis and laid out the scheme.

"I should concur with you in accepting these terms but for the constitutional difficulty," Davis responded. "You know that Congress has no jurisdiction over the subject of slavery."

Lyons quickly concocted a solution. "Let the bill providing for the gradual abolition of slavery also provide that it shall not take effect until the States have, by acts of their respective legislatures, duly passed, approved and ratified it," he said. If Davis agreed to the plan, Lyons said he would "introduce the bill tomorrow."

"Well, I must consult the Cabinet," Davis replied, "and if they agree with you I will send for you." Lyons never heard back on the matter.

In late September 1862, President Lincoln proposed his Emancipation Proclamation. Suddenly, the South feared slave uprisings more than ever. Lincoln's Proclamation not only declared slaves free but also called on them to "abstain from all violence, *unless* in necessary defense" (italics added). Just days later, Lyons made an impassioned speech to the Confederate Congress, calling it "the most inhuman and atrocious…[proclamation] that was ever issued by any man or power professing to be civilized." He railed at this attempt "to incite servile insurrection against us" and proposed ruthless measures against slaves who revolted.

Now that the issue of slavery was front and center in the war, the French and English reversed course on intervention. Lyons was surely crushed. His diplomacy had failed.

——◦◦◦——

As the war dragged on, the Confederate Congress debated getting tougher with Union men—unconditionally killing them on sight if in Confederate territory. In keeping with this sentiment, James Lyons proposed a resolution urging Confederate citizens to "kill and destroy" all Union military personnel unless they were "a regular prisoner of war" and stated that after January 1, 1863, "no officer of the Lincolnite Army or Navy ought to be captured alive, and if so captured, he ought to be immediately hung." Lyons even suggested "offering a bounty of $20 and an annuity of $20 for life to every slave and free negro" who killed "one of the enemy." After a months-long debate in the Confederate Congress, a joint resolution was passed that focused its wrath on Union officers leading black troops, since they were "deemed as inciting servile insurrection."[41]

——◦◦◦——

On the frigid evening of Saturday, February 7, 1863, James and Imogen Lyons hosted French-born General Polignac at Laburnum for dinner. On the guest list were three more Confederate generals—Sterling Price, Charles Clark and William Booth Taliaferro. Other dignitaries included former governor of Mississippi Henry Stuart Foote and William Porcher Miles of South Carolina. While many Richmonders were suffering deep deprivation that winter, the privileged Lyonses served "a very fine dinner." Afterward, in true Southern fashion, the ladies excused themselves to the parlor and "speeches and sentiments" began among the men. The "soul of hospitality," Mr. Lyons offered a toast to Polignac's homeland. Flattered, Polignac praised his adoptive country, which he called, "the promised land of [his] youthful dreams," for which he "would be proud to die."

That same winter, the Lyonses hosted another unforgettable soiree. The guests included Mary Chesnut, the vivacious Civil War diarist, whose husband was a military aide to President Davis. At dinner, Chesnut was seated next to "a clever unknown" whose name she didn't catch. The dark and intense gentleman seemed well connected and knowledgeable, and she found his opinions "incisive" and "decisive." At one point, he began speaking in epigrams. "Don't try that style!" Chesnut blurted. "That is like the *Examiner*."

Craftily, the gentleman teased her. He asked, "Do you include the *Examiner* among those newspapers you denounce as giving aid and comfort to…the Yankees?"

"Yes," Chesnut replied, "they are splitting us into a thousand pieces." She vilified editors of newspapers like the *Examiner* for railing against President Davis's conduct of the war—intimating that the *Examiner*'s editor should be hanged for fostering disunity. She proclaimed, "If I were a shouting character, I should say, 'Three cheers for the gentlemen privates! To the lantern for the dissenting editors!'" Toward the end of the evening, while in the Laburnum drawing room, Mary learned that her table companion was none other than John Moncure Daniel, the editor of the *Examiner*.

In March 1863, while the Confederates found themselves in a swirl of difficult challenges—including Lincoln's new Conscription Act—Lyons received a compliment in the *Richmond Dispatch*. "The Hon. James Lyons, of Henrico County, will be supported for our next Governor," said the blurb. "He is the man to carry us through our troubles." It was signed, simply, "Many Voters."[42] Lyons didn't pursue a run for the governor's office because he was trying to keep his seat in the Confederate House of Representatives. But in the May 28 election, he lost to Williams C. Wickham, who'd scored points for forming a cavalry company for the cause.

Lyons was soon as busy as ever with his law practice, sometimes teaming up with George Wythe Randolph, Thomas Jefferson's grandson. The high-powered Lyons served as defense counsel for accused murderers, traitors and extortionists.[43]

———◦•◦———

On the evening of January 22, 1864, Lyons flocked with other Richmonders to the First African Church on Broad Street. Everyone gathered to discuss supplying "artificial limbs for all officers and soldiers and seamen who have been maimed in the service of their country."[44] Forming the Association for the Relief of Maimed Soldiers, they adopted a constitution, elected officers for one year and collected large donations. James Lyons was elected one of the group's twelve vice-presidents.[45]

At about 10:00 a.m. on a dark and rainy March 1, while Lyons was at home, he probably feared bodily harm himself. He could hear artillery fire at dangerously close range. It was the infamous Dahlgren-Kilpatrick raid, storming the outskirts of the Confederate capitol. A column of 3,000 to 5,000 Union cavalry had penetrated the city's outer fortifications, and artillerymen had set up several cannon on a farm less than a mile north of Laburnum—the site of today's Bellevue Court neighborhood.[46] They then advanced toward the city to engage the Confederates at the intermediate fortifications, located just about five hundred feet north of the Laburnum mansion.[47] The Confederates swept into action. Colonel Walter H. Stevens hastily pulled together 380 men,[48] who pushed forward light and heavy artillery and then fired. A deadly volley forced the Confederates back to the shelter of the intermediate fortifications, but they eventually drove Kilpatrick's force back. One rebel was killed, and seven were wounded.[49]

On March 1, 1864, thousands of Federal troops pressed on the intermediate fortifications on Brook Turnpike, which were lightly manned. Quickly, Confederate general Walter H. Stevens scrounged up 380 reserves. By necessity, they were mostly young department clerks and citizens. *The Photographic History of the Civil War.*

In the middle of the battle, one or two Union shells landed on the Laburnum lawn. Lyons panicked. He rushed to Jefferson Davis's office and reported that the enemy was shelling his house. But the battle only lasted about two hours.[50] The Union troops had retreated because their larger plot fell apart. Two Union officers, Ulric Dahlgren and H. Judson Kilpatrick, had intended to penetrate the city of Richmond—Dahlgren from the south and Kilpatrick from the north. Once united, they intended to free hundreds of Union prisoners, kill President Davis and his cabinet and torch Richmond. But before Dahlgren could reach the city, he was killed in an ambush. Richmond was saved for now—as was Laburnum.

But just two weeks later, in the middle of the night, fire broke out at the mansion. Asleep on the second floor were James Lyons, his wife and two of his grown daughters from a former marriage. "Every room in the house was filled with smoke before any one was aroused," reported the *Dispatch*, "and on awakening they had barely time to escape in their night dresses." Trying to save whatever he could, Lyons returned to the burning building, suffered a bad fall and knocked out several teeth. He watched as his glorious home was consumed by flames. "With the exception of a few trifling articles of furniture," said the *Dispatch*, all of the mansion's finery was destroyed, including Mr. Lyons's "magnificent law library, that cannot be replaced in the Confederacy," and "valued at over $30,000."[51] Also lost were costly portraits and Imogen's diamonds.

A few days later, Varina Davis took a carriage to Laburnum with Mary Chesnut to check on the Lyons family. "It was really pitiful," Chesnut wrote. "Only a few days before, we had been there…and found them all taking tea under those beautiful shade trees. And now—smoke and ashes—nothing more."

The day after the blaze, the *Dispatch* reported that "the fire was the work of an incendiary." There were two theories. "One is that a large pile of shavings and other combustible matter was placed under the house in several places and then set fire to, while another has it that on the back porch, immediately against the door, the incendiary applied his torch."[52] Although no proof was ever offered, Lyons assumed the arsonist was Wilson, a neighbor's mulatto slave living at Laburnum. Wilson had recently admitted that he knew where Billy was hiding but wouldn't divulge his whereabouts, so Lyons took him to court for "conniving at" Billy's escape. During the hearing, Lyons lost his temper, warning that "if the negro…ever put his foot upon his plantation again he would administer to him his breakfast or dinner in the shape of a load of buckshot." But the judge found insufficient evidence to proceed and ordered Wilson's release. That was the very day before the fire. It seems James Lyons's racial attitudes may have finally caught up with him.

With the Laburnum mansion only a memory, Lyons moved his family into a small cottage on the property. Just a month later, Imogen wrote a friend that "you would really be surprised to see how bright & comfortable the old cottage looks." She and her husband even managed to entertain the Davises there for dinner.

The following winter, Lyons extended a special kindness to Varina Davis. Finding her family in financial difficulty, she had just sold two of her horses to a dealer. That very afternoon, Lyons and a few other prominent gentlemen bought back the two horses and returned them to her stable with a note, begging her to accept the gift in token of their regard.[53]

In early 1865, a desperate shortage of Confederate troops forced a debate over arming the slaves. "Virginius" resurfaced in the pages of the *Enquirer*. He denounced the act as evil but acknowledged that the public supported it.[54]

On Sunday, April 2, right after church services, the most alarming news hit the streets of Richmond. General Lee's lines had been broken at Petersburg, and the Confederate government was packing up to flee the capital. Since James Lyons was an original secessionist, his friends warned that the Federals might "arrest him the first man, and hang him."[55]

Like a horrible plague, word spread that everyone must evacuate the city by midnight. One anxious Richmond lady sought out James Lyons to see if it was all true. He said there was "no use in further evading the truth."

The lady asked him what he was going to do. "I shall stand my ground," Lyons told her. "I have a sick family, and we must take our chances together."

"Then seriously, really and truly, Richmond is to be given up, after all, to the enemy?" she wailed.

"Nothing less!" Lyons replied. "And we are going to have a rough time, I imagine."[56]

Lyons was right. The city fell into absolute chaos and pandemonium as citizens and government officials planned their escapes, and a tremendous fire swept through the commercial district. The city's leaders knew what had to be done. A small group of men, including Mayor Mayo and James Lyons's son, Judge William H. Lyons, set out in a dilapidated hack for the city's eastern outskirts to surrender the capitol. Finally, the parties came face to face. Judge Lyons greeted the Union men and handed them the surrender note, which, due to the paper shortage, was written on the back of a piece of floral wallpaper.[57] "Judge Lyons could not have performed the honours of introduction between the municipal party and the Federal officers with statelier grace," said one source.[58] The fruit hadn't fallen far from the tree.

With the war over, James Lyons's slaves were free men. He resumed his law practice, and given time, his fortunes would rebound.

But Lyons didn't take the new order sitting down. In the harrowing days of Reconstruction, he remained a firebrand. In August 1865, he attended a large public gathering at the Capitol and made a statement that some thought imprudent. He said the Yankees had destroyed slavery and he "wished to God" they would take all the black people as well.

Two years later, Lyons voluntarily served on the defense team in one of the most sensational trials in American history. It was the treason trial of his "dear beloved friend and leader" Jefferson Davis, who'd just spent two hellish years in Federal prison. On May 13, 1867, a pale and haggard Davis entered a crowded courtroom in the Custom House at Eleventh and Bank Streets in Richmond—the very building that housed his wartime office. During the proceedings, he was released on $100,000 bail, with James Lyons among the signers of the bail bond. Moments later, Lyons escorted Davis out of the building, as hundreds of people cheered jubilantly in the streets.

Months later, Lyons invited his co-counsel on the Davis case to the Laburnum estate for an auspicious dinner. Those present also included United States District Attorney Beach and Chief Justice Salmon P. Chase, a former Confederate soldier. Apparently meeting in the cottage on the property, they strategized legal maneuvers to keep Jefferson Davis's case from going to trial. This took place just one day before the "illustrious prisoner" was released for good.[59]

It was Christmas Day 1868 when Davis was granted amnesty by President Andrew Johnson. Lyons had made an appeal to Johnson on Davis's behalf. For the rest of James Lyons's life, he and Davis remained close, writing heartfelt letters to each other. In some of them, Lyons counseled Davis on clearing his name.

The old Laburnum property was purchased in 1883 by another distinguished Richmond lawyer, Joseph Bryan. He built his own spectacular Laburnum mansion, a Stick-influenced brick Victorian. It burned in 1906. In 1908, he built another grand Laburnum in classical style, which still stands.

In 1909, the year after this third Laburnum was completed, a new book offered reminiscences of wartime Richmond. Titled *Belles, Beaux and Brains of the Sixties*, author Thomas Cooper DeLeon said, "Today no habitué writes or speaks of the giddy and long-guarded capital without mention of the Lyons home."[60]

Chapter 5

BLOODY CARAVAN FROM SEVEN PINES

Richmond Becomes One Vast Hospital

To many Richmonders, the war mission was one of glory and excitement, accompanied by patriotic tunes from a marching band. That is, until mid-May 1862. The Federal army had inched up the Virginia Peninsula just seven short miles from the city, filling the citizens with terror. "We in Richmond had begun to feel like the prisoner of the Inquisition in Poe's story, cast into a dungeon of slowly contracting walls," said auburn-haired Constance Cary, then nineteen years old. Many citizens, believing that the Confederate authorities would decide to evacuate the city, departed southward by the trainload. Even Jefferson Davis's wife and children fled.

On May 31, stalwart Richmonders could hear the sound of cannon and musket fire from the east at Seven Pines. "Every heart leaped as if deliverance were at hand," Constance said, since most families in the city had a father, son or brother there standing in staunch defense. The city dwellers swiftly made preparations for the wounded. But they had no concept of the massive onslaught to come. Over the next three days, five thousand bloodied, war-torn men would arrive in Richmond for urgent care.

It all began on the morning of June 1. "Ambulances, litters, carts, every vehicle that the city could produce, went and came with a ghastly burden," Constance described vividly. "Those who could walk limped painfully home, in some cases so black with gunpowder they passed unrecognized. Women with pallid faces flitted bareheaded through the streets searching for their dead or wounded... Men too old or infirm to fight went on horseback or

With wounded soldiers filling the streets, city dwellers helped however they could.
Illustration by Richmonder, William L. Sheppard, who saw action at Seven Pines with the
Richmond Howitzers. *Battles and Leaders of the Civil War.*

afoot to meet the returning ambulances, and in some cases served as escort
to their own dying sons."

Many of the men had shattered limbs. By that afternoon, the hot
streets of Richmond became one massive emergency room. It was
sheer bedlam. Many citizens, including the ladies, tended the soldiers as
best they could. Slaves helped, too. Then space had to be found in the
crowded city for care of the wounded—whether in stores, warehouses,
hotels or private homes.

Meanwhile, two girls were looking desperately for a member of their
family reported wounded. Constance kindly offered to help. The three
darted among the wounded, from "one scene of honor to another." Finally
they decided to look at the old St. Charles Hotel, at the northeast corner of
Main and Wall (Fifteenth). With the hotel business suspended, the building
had been used as a war hospital since First Manassas the previous summer.
As Constance and the girls walked through the door of the plain, four-story
brick building, the cool indoor air momentarily refreshed them. The next
instant, they were hit by the gloomiest of spectacles: "Men in every stage of
mutilation lying on the bare boards, with perhaps a haversack or an army
blanket beneath their heads,—some dying, all suffering keenly, while waiting

their turn to be attended to. To be there empty-handed and impotent nearly broke our hearts. We passed from one to the other, making such slight additions to their comfort as were possible."

Many patients shared the fate of eighteen-year-old Isaac Augustus Hughes, who died just days later. It didn't help that the hospital was grossly understaffed and, according to several neighbors, "in an insufferably filthy condition."[61] Regardless, many more war-torn soldiers would be rushed to the St. Charles Hospital that summer.

It was the warm morning of June 30, the sixth day of the Seven Days' Battles around Richmond. Seventeen-year-old Randolph Abbott Shotwell was on the march to Frayser's Farm just east of the Confederate capital with the Eighth Virginia Regiment. His worn-out boots had fallen apart, and his bare feet were painful and swollen from the rocky terrain. He dearly hoped to meet up with his older brother, Hamilton, who was following close behind with the Thirty-fourth North Carolina. They'd seen each other only once in the last three years. Randolph discreetly lagged behind his regiment a bit to begin his search. But before long, Confederate cavalry galloped past him, reporting that the enemy was at a stand not far in front. He hustled back to his place in line.

That hot and sultry afternoon, Randolph and his comrades took position to the left of Long Bridge Road near Frayser's Farm. Artillerymen positioned a four-gun battery in a small clearing on the side of the road and fired a signal to General "Stonewall" Jackson. In a flash, a Federal storm of shot and shell rained on their regiment. "Almost in an instant the deadly missiles were hurtling through the woods, cutting off the treetops, crashing here, there, and everywhere," Randolph described. "Sometimes a feathery top of a tall pine sapling would be cut off, and descending like an arrow or javelin impale and transfix to the earth any poor wretch so unlucky as to be beneath." As a consolation, the Federal gunners were unaware of their position and firing at random.

Then, at around five o'clock, with the enemy a mile ahead, Randolph's regiment charged forward in a full run. Randolph kept up as long as he could, but his feet were in agony. Finally he broke down. Managing to inch his way back to the battery, he volunteered to work the gun. But minutes later, the

Federals advanced, so the battery abandoned its position. Randolph moved to the forest's edge, waiting for his regiment to retreat. The guns fell quiet.

Randolph waited and waited, but his comrades didn't come back. He had no idea where they were, either. Guessing they might return later in a retrograde movement, he decided to bivouac along the roadside for the night. Besides, he hoped to reconnect with his brother, who'd probably been in the battle.

Before long, a soldier from his brother's unit happened by. The news wasn't good. "The Thirty-fourth is cut all to pieces," the soldier reported. "Lieutenant Shotwell had his leg torn square off with a shell!" Randolph dropped his musket, staring in disbelief. The soldier didn't know any more details, except that Hamilton had been carried off the field and probably taken to Richmond.

With dusk fast approaching, Randolph immediately took off for the city, desperate to find his brother. Along the way, he searched at the roadside field hospitals. He was horrified by the grisly scenes, where crude tables had been set up for amputations. "Severed arms, legs, hands, feet, eyes, and other fragments of the human frame lay in piles like cordwood," he described. Corpses lay nearby.

With no sign of Hamilton anywhere, Randolph resumed his journey. After walking for miles, he collapsed from exhaustion. Little did he know he was fast asleep in the grass along the road's edge, near a turnoff. Hours later, he was awakened by a violent clatter. Peering up, he saw a full regiment of Confederate cavalry galloping right past him—the hooves pounding the dusty road just two feet from his head. The cavalry couldn't see him in the dark.

By dawn, he was back on the road, amazed he was still in one piece. He knew that pickets could pick him up for straggling from his regiment.

Randolph's sense of duty was strong—but today, the "call of affection" was stronger. Besides, he and his brother had made a pact. If either of them was ever wounded, the other would rush to his aid—no matter what. As Randolph put one throbbing foot in front of the other, he reminisced about the day their pact was sealed.

It was about a month earlier, at a long-awaited reunion at Hamilton's camp on the Mechanicsville Pike near Richmond. The moment their eyes met, they ran to each other and hugged tight. Hamilton was a sight for sore eyes. Always "lithe, graceful, neat and handsome," he looked "unusually well in his dark blue suit, trimmed with gold braid, and with cap and band to match." It was a joyous reunion. The brothers talked and talked, catching up

Alexander Hamilton Shotwell, pictured early in the war. A religious man devoted to the Confederate cause, he believed that God would "bring order out of this chaos—even though it may be at the expense of my life and happiness." *Portraits of Conflict: A Photographic History of North Carolina in the Civil War.*.

on everything that had happened over the past three years. For time alone, they strolled up the hillside and sat upon a mighty iron siege-gun, its muzzle overlooking the green, grassy valley of the Chickahominy. Below lay the Meadow Bridge. On the south side of the stream were grey-clad pickets, and a stone's throw away were their counterparts in blue.

"I suspect we shall lead an attack on those white camps over yonder before many days," Hamilton said ominously. "Let us have it as an understanding that so long as we are in the vicinity of one another, either one who gets sick, or is wounded shall promptly notify the other, who will drop everything, and hasten to his assistance."

"Agreed, I will come, or would come were there any need," Randolph replied, "but I have no idea I shall be summoned, and certainly God grant I may not be!" The brothers spent the evening chatting in the strawberry gardens nearby, enjoying the delicious berries and lolling in the grass.

With these warm memories flooding his mind, Randolph trudged into the outskirts of Richmond. Things were getting very dangerous now. He was away without leave, and pickets guarded the roads entering the city. Skulking behind fences and dodging down gullies, he finally reached the northern part of Rocketts Wharf. Without catching his breath, he began his search through the hospitals. The scenes were gruesome and frightful. "Room after room presented the same shocking spectacle of row after row of cots, whereon lay pale, bloody, ghastly, mangled remains of what a few days previous were stalwart men!" Randolph described. "Men with bandaged heads, men with sightless eyes, men without arms, without legs, with broken shoulders, with bullet-riddled bodies—all suffering, groaning—and in many instances dying!"

After searching the hospitals for two days, Randolph was walking down a third-floor corridor of the St. Charles Hospital. "This way, brother!" he heard Hamilton utter feebly. Entering the small, hot, crowded room, he saw Hamilton lying on a cot. He rushed to his bedside, speechless. Looking up, Hamilton said, "Pretty badly damaged, brother, and I've suffered a good deal more than I ever imagined one could suffer, but I am doing rather better since my leg was taken off."

It was even worse than Randolph expected. An explosive bullet had struck his brother's kneecap and shattered the bone above and below the knee. As Randolph took a peek at Hamilton's leg, sympathy quickly gave over to rage. Incompetent "surgeon-butchers" had made fast work of slashing off the leg. It was cut square off, with bone protruding two inches beyond the flesh—and the wound wasn't even stitched up. Randolph fumed. This was little less than murder, he thought. The entire end of the gory limb was infected with maggots. And to make matters worse, there was only one male nurse in the room for twelve patients. Randolph left the room to collect himself.

When he returned, Hamilton had two army friends by his side. One was Captain Joe C. Mills of the Second South Carolina, who had rushed there after hearing the news. The other was Tom Carson, one of the men who'd helped carry Hamilton off the battlefield.

Hamilton decided that Carson should take over as nurse. He insisted that Randolph return to camp, so he wouldn't be sought for as a deserter.

———◦◦———

When Randolph came to visit the following day, Hamilton had a raging fever. Their anxious father, Reverend Nathan Shotwell, burst in the room from North Carolina. After taking a look at Hamilton and his amputated leg, he reacted with the same rage as Randolph had.

Then came a ray of hope. Captain Mills found a room for Hamilton in the home of Samuel H. Taylor about a mile from the city. Hamilton was far too weak to take a bumpy ride by horse-drawn ambulance, so he was carried on a litter by Randolph, Captain Mills, Tom Carson and a "colored servant" named George. As they paced in unison all the way to the Taylor home, Reverend Shotwell carefully held an umbrella to shield his boy from the sun.

When they arrived at the house, several wounded officers were already there, so the "noble ladies" providing care made room on the second floor. Hamilton seemed to perk up almost as soon as he arrived in his fresh surroundings. His cot was near a "latticed window, shaded by blooming honeysuckles, and rendered cheerful by the twittering of canary birds, and vases of flowers." The scene couldn't have been more different from the St. Charles Hospital, with its lice, swarms of flies, foul odors and noisy commotion. This room was cool and quiet—with the scent of fresh flowers, no less.

Before long, Dr. Edgerton of Hamilton's command came by. He would provide Hamilton almost constant care.

On Sunday, July 6, Randolph once again slipped away from camp to check on his brother. Shortly after he arrived, more of Hamilton's comrades came to visit. The patient was cheerful and talkative but lamented that his career as an officer was over. He almost wept, knowing he would never again lead his friends in battle.

Randolph spent that night in a chair by his brother's side.

Just before dawn, Hamilton awoke. "Brother, my leg is bleeding again, I think," he said. There was a pool of blood in the bed. Randolph ran to get Dr. Edgerton. They quickly fashioned a tourniquet out of a handkerchief, then Dr. Edgerton fled to Richmond to get help. Hamilton was talking, feebly but calmly. He was very sad that he would be leaving his young wife and infant son—a son he'd never seen. Just then, Reverend Shotwell entered the room, visibly devastated by his son's pallid appearance.

As Hamilton got weaker and weaker, he seemed to be at peace with his fate. With his sobbing father bending over the bed, Hamilton turned to him and said, "I rather expected to go home with you, but now I shall not." He then corrected himself, saying, "Yes, I'll go with you but not as I expected!" Moments later, twenty-three-year-old Hamilton Shotwell was dead.

Reverend Shotwell knelt by the bed, peering longingly at his son's still face. The doctors from Richmond ran into the room. It was too late.

Needless to say, Randolph and his father were heartbroken. But they took some comfort in the fact that Hamilton had died a hero. On June 30, during the Seven Days' Battles, Pender's North Carolina Brigade was sent in pursuit of McClellan and ended up capturing a "powerful battery of Napoleon guns." Exultant, Hamilton was standing upon "the limber chest of one of the captured cannon, making a congratulatory speech to encourage the men." Moments later came surprise fire from a "fresh line of Yankees," and Hamilton fell. A half dozen of his comrades threw down their guns to carry him off the field, but he "nobly bade them resume their weapons, and advance into the fight," saying their first duty was to defeat the foe. Hamilton may have survived if he hadn't been so selfless.

General Pender had commended Hamilton for action performed just two days before receiving his fatal wound. "Lieutenant Hamilton Shotwell cannot be spoken of too highly, for his gallant conduct," he said. In the face of "heavy and murderous cross fire," Hamilton had run along the front of the regiment, taken a color-bearer by the arm and rushed him to the front, shouting, "All that will stand by the flag, come on!" As General Pender put it, Hamilton's conspicuous gallantry encouraged "the men to move forward at a very critical moment."

Now, sadly, Randolph and his father needed a coffin for their brave loved one. They set out to Richmond for the grim task. As before, Randolph was careful not to be noticed, lest he be picked up as a deserter. Late that afternoon, having succeeded with their mission, the men arrived at the Richmond and Petersburg Station at Eighth and Byrd Streets, bearing their beloved Hamilton in a coffin. Reverend Shotwell was to accompany his son's remains back home to North Carolina. In the shuffle, he realized his suitcase had been stolen. This heaped tragedy upon tragedy, since the suitcase held mementos intended for Hamilton's wife and child—his sword belt, pistol, papers and letters.

Late the next morning, the train finally pulled out of the grimy station and puffed southward over the James River. Randolph could see his father standing at the door of a baggage car, in tears. As soon as the train disappeared from sight, Randolph slowly turned and began his long walk back to camp.

He would carry on his duties with the hundreds of other men—a lonely soul just the same.

Chapter 6

VIOLET'S WAR

Tragedy and Mayhem in the Countryside

T he Yankees had upped their ante, stealing everything that wasn't nailed down—horses, mules, carriages, local crops and even slaves. It was March 1864, and Yankees were waging a cavalry raid in the northern outskirts of the Capital of the Confederacy.

But first, let's go back three years earlier, shortly before Virginia seceded, when the area was rocked by gunfire and murder. The victim was a thirty-five-year-old man named John Oscar Taylor.

Mr. Taylor, his wife, Tremanda, and their nine-year old daughter lived on a 118-acre farm worked by slaves. With cows, hogs and a stable of horses, it was bordered on the east by the Brook Turnpike, today's Brook Road, and on the north by Mill Road, today's Westbrook Avenue.[62] The Taylors' farmhouse was nestled along a stream near the intersection of today's Newport Drive and Lorraine Avenue.[63] A stone's throw to the north was "Westbrook," a plantation home then occupied by John B. Young. He was a prominent lawyer and prosecutor for the Commonwealth, and in a few short months, he would sign Virginia's Ordinance of Secession.

On the afternoon of January 11, 1861, Mr. Taylor was in high spirits, working at another farm he'd recently acquired on the site of today's Bryan Parkway neighborhood. An elderly man walked up on the scene. He was Joseph Bernard, the man who'd sold him the farm. The two got into an argument about rights to a slave girl named Violet, and Bernard shot Taylor in the abdomen. The bullet lodged in his spine, and he fell to the ground, writhing in pain.[64]

One of the first to learn of the shooting was the overseer of John B. Young's plantation, who fled to Westbrook with the news. Young rushed to Taylor's side at the Young's Pond mill house, where doctors were tending the wound. Taylor recounted the whole lurid tale, and Young—well versed in the law—wrote everything down word for word. He knew it could be used in court later.

Over the next two weeks, Mr. Taylor lay at home in agony, his life hanging by a thread. Then, on January 27, he died.[65]

Prosecuting the case against Bernard was none other than John B. Young of Westbrook. On the defense team was another prominent Richmond attorney, James Lyons.[66] The handsomest man of his day, he was master of Laburnum on the Brook Turnpike and would soon be elected a member of the Confederate Congress.

When the war broke out, Bernard was languishing in a Henrico County prison cell. His violent tendencies resurfaced. That June, he wrote a letter to newly elected Confederate president Jefferson Davis. Using James Lyons as a reference, he said he had a plan to destroy Yankee forts with a bombshell. He wanted testing to be done and hoped it could be kept secret.[67]

Bernard's trial began that October, shortly after the first bloodbath of the war at Manassas. He was found guilty of the lesser charge of manslaughter, perhaps because he'd endeared himself to the Rebels.[68]

Now a grieving widow, Mrs. Taylor faced cold, harsh realities. She auctioned off some of her belongings, even offering a few of her slaves up for hire. But she kept the house and some of the slaves to work the farm.[69]

In the spring of 1863, one of her male slaves ran away. She offered twenty-five dollars for the return of a man named Dick, "about five feet six inches in height, gingerbread color," with "a lump on the shoulders."[70]

It was a year after Mrs. Taylor ran that ad that the Yankee cavalry raid wreaked havoc in her section of the countryside. It was all part of a much bigger plot known as the Dahlgren-Kilpatrick Raid. These two generals planned to penetrate the city of Richmond from two sides on March 1, 1864, free hundreds of Yankee prisoners, kill President Davis and his cabinet and torch Richmond.

That morning, according to plan, General Kilpatrick's division approached the northern outskirts of Richmond along the Brook Turnpike. After clearing the city's Outer Defenses, Kilpatrick "sent forward a detachment with eight pieces of cannon" and "formed a line of battle on Mrs. Taylor's farm."[71] They commenced an artillery duel with troops at the intermediate fortifications. A shell landed on the lawn at the Laburnum mansion but caused no damage.

Mischief maker, Union general H. Judson Kilpatrick.
He ruthlessly took the war to the local citizenry.
Portraits of Conflict: A Photographic History of North Carolina in the Civil War.

About 4:00 that afternoon, the Rebels drove the Yankees into retreat, but not before one Rebel had been killed and seven others wounded.[72]

By the time it was all over, the Yankees had seized dozens of horses and mules from Mrs. Taylor's neighboring farms. From the Brook Hill Plantation, they reportedly took all of John Stewart's horses, mules and bacon and consumed or destroyed "fifty barrels of corn, a large quantity of wheat and oats, and other articles." Continuing their rampage in the area, they stole buggies and slaves, rifled through "drawers and wardrobes" and took a poor widow's only horse. At Westbrook, they took not only all of John B. Young's mules, horses and his "negro butler," but they also reportedly captured Mr. Young himself. Apparently, he was released soon thereafter.[73]

About a year later, in early April 1865, Richmond was in fact torched—but by the Rebels themselves. They set fire to the tobacco warehouses near the river because the Yankees were about to capture the Confederate capitol, and General Lee didn't want the Yankees to benefit from the tobacco. As the Rebels evacuated the city, the fire spread to engulf at least twenty square blocks.

With that, all the slaves—including Violet—were free at last. And as for Mrs. Taylor, she was left to pick up the pieces yet again.

Chapter 7

CHEERS AT THE RICHMOND THEATRE

Culture Amid the Chaos

I t seemed the world had gone mad, especially for the people of Richmond. Their once-peaceful and prosperous city had become ground zero in the War Between the States. Inflation skyrocketed 9,000 percent. There were shortages of just about everything—everything, that is, except dead and maimed Confederate soldiers. The Federals had drawn a giant bull's-eye on the city, and the reality of its capture inched closer by the week. What the people of Richmond desperately needed was an escape. Some, no doubt, drowned their sorrows in booze.

Others just went to the theater. The city had been the entertainment mecca of the South for years, drawing nationally famous actors like Edwin Booth, Joe Jefferson and Edwin Forrest. There was a steady menu of first-rate tragedies, comedies, minstrel shows, farces and operas. By taking in a show, Richmonders felt their world was civilized, if only for a couple of hours.

The city's most prestigious venue, at the southeast corner of Seventh and Broad Streets, was the Richmond Theatre. The 1819 structure was simply called "The Theatre," and its company "successfully catered to the refined tastes of the lovers of the drama." The tracks of the Richmond, Fredericksburg and Potomac Railroad ran right by the building, down the center of Broad Street, and trains unloaded theatergoers from neighboring towns.

In November 1861, the theater opened for the season—war or no war. One night it held a benefit for war refugees "from that once beautiful but now desolated town" of Hampton, Virginia.[74] And in December, it featured a young

The Richmond Theatre stood tall on Broad Street at Seventh. This scene could pass for wartime, except for the Stars and Stripes flying from the rooftop. *VCU Libraries.*

Ida Vernon in the classic *Romeo and Juliet*. But on New Year's night, the theater was the scene of a gripping, real-life drama. It caught fire and burned to the ground, destroying the company's musical instruments, stage scenery, costumes and sheet music.

Even as the war raged in 1862, rebuilding began. By year's end, the exterior was completed, its front adorned by four Corinthian columns. Then, on February 9, 1863, the new Richmond Theatre's rich crimson curtain—decorated with cords and fringes—opened to Shakespeare's *As You Like It* in five acts.

Without question, one of the biggest hits throughout the war was a musical titled *The Virginia Cavalier*. It was especially popular among soldiers passing through the city because of its young star, Miss Sallie Partington. Fancying themselves as Bob Roebuck, the "darling of her heart," they cheered "Miss Sallie! Miss Sallie!" whenever she sang, "The Southern Soldier Boy":

Bob Roebuck is my sweetheart's name
He's off to the wars and gone
He's fighting for his Nannie dear
His sword is buckled on

He's fighting for his own true love
His foes he does defy
He is the darling of my heart
My Southern soldier boy

Oh if in battle he was slain
I'm sure that I should die
but I'm sure he'll come again
And cheer my weeping eye

But should he fall
In this our glorious cause
He still would be my joy
For many a sweetheart mourns the loss
Of a Southern soldier boy

I hope for the best
And so do all
Whose hopes are in the field
I know that we shall win the day
For Southerns never yield

And when we think
Of those who are away
We'll look above for joy
And I'm mighty glad
That my Bobby is
A Southern soldier boy

A local girl, Sallie was well known for her love of the Southern Confederacy. "In Richmond her name was a toast," said one newspaper, "In the camps she was an idol."[75]

The Virginia Cavalier also dished out an exciting spectacle. A horse and rider galloped right across the stage, with the rider dressed in a black provost

Alexander's monster of a dog, Nero. Some described him as fierce, while others said he was a pussycat. *The Soldier's Story.*

marshal's uniform and a gigantic black dog barking at his heels. The scene sparked "vociferous" applause. The man in the role had actually written the play and even the tender lyrics to "The Southern Soldier Boy." But this was hardly his only gig in town. Ironically, he was the iron-fisted commandant of Castle Thunder prison. He'd named the prison himself, wanting "its very name to be a terror to evil-doers."[76]

His name was Captain George W. Alexander, and the black dog was his fierce Bavarian boar hound "Nero." Reportedly, the dog weighed a monstrous 182 pounds.[77] Some Richmonders recognized the dog from the city streets. "Ordinarily he was good natured, playful, and docile," said one citizen, "but when angered or provoked he was terrible looking, and dangerous. I have seen Captain Alexander whip him with a horsewhip, at the same time have a cocked revolver in his other hand, which occasionally he would fire over his head, and then he appeared the very impersonation of ferocity subdued by the will of man."[78]

Richmonders knew well that in June 1861, Alexander helped seize the steamer *St. Nicholas*, which, as it was plying from Washington to Baltimore laden with valuable commodities, was entered by Captain Alexander and more than twenty other men, all in disguise as passengers. One of them wore a hoop skirt and veil, fluttering a fan. At the right moment, they threw off their disguises, buckled on swords and pistols and captured the officers and crew. It was part of a bigger plan to weaken the Union navy. Although it didn't go as planned, it managed to bag three small commercial vessels loaded with coffee and ice—luxuries by this time.

Richmonders also knew that a short time afterward, Alexander was captured by the Federal forces in Maryland and jailed in Fort McHenry near Baltimore and made a daring escape a few months later. The plan was concocted by his "true, noble, courageous little wife." She got permission to visit him at Fort McHenry and carried a Federal uniform and an "inflating life-preserving waistcoat" under her dress.

Tough on the outside, prison commandant George W. Alexander also wrote plays with tender lyrics. *The Woman In Battle.*

Just after dark, he donned his disguise and slipped out of his cell. While a fellow inmate distracted the sentinel, Alexander jumped over the wall into a ditch, scratched his way to the river, inflated his waistcoat and swam to Baltimore. Eventually making his way to Richmond, he was "received with great cordiality by Governor Letcher," and soon thereafter, General Winder appointed him assistant provost marshal of Richmond and commander of Castle Thunder Prison.[79] Alexander seemed like the perfect man for the job, since he'd been a prisoner of war himself.

Despite Alexander's flair for swashbuckling heroics, he didn't get the same adoration as sweet Sallie Partington. He had enemies. And they would soon get him into hot water with the Confederate government.

Castle Thunder opened in August 1862. Before long, it was crowded with Confederate deserters, male political prisoners, women, African Americans and even Federal deserters and prisoners of war. By January 1863, the Castle was at twice its capacity, with three thousand prisoners.

Almost from the start, Alexander gained a reputation for brutality. As a commandant, he was described as "harsh, inhuman, tyrannical, and dishonest in every possible way."[80] But the inmates were no angels either. Many were

Alexander's punishments included barrel shirts, or "the wooden overcoat." *Hardtack and Coffee.*

hardened criminals "of very bad repute" and habitually robbed and beat other inmates. Others tried to bribe the prison guards or escape. Once, some prisoners even set off a large explosion of gunpowder.

The question was whether Alexander's punishments fit the crimes. Some prisoners were tied up by their thumbs for up to eight hours, with their toes barely touching the floor. Some wore barrel shirts. Some were branded. And Confederate deserters were often given fifty lashes across their bare backs or sent to Camp Lee for execution. While these were common practices for the time, Castle Thunder stood alone among soldiers and would-be deserters. An army ballad proclaimed:

I'd ruther be on the Grandfather
  Mountain
A-taking the snow and rain
Than to be in Castle Thunder
A-wearin' the ball and chain.

By early 1863, Alexander's enemies among the civilians of Richmond tried to topple him—bringing his treatment of prisoners at Castle Thunder to the attention of the Confederate Congress. That April, the Confederate Congress appointed a special committee to investigate the management of Castle Thunder. The hearings lasted nineteen days. In the end, the committee concluded that Alexander's methods, although unusual, "were not cruel under the circumstances, but were allowable and necessary for the preservation of good order and obedience in the prison."[81]

But Alexander wasn't off the hook yet. That December, his enemies brought more charges against him—this time for extorting large sums of money from prisoners in return for assurances of freedom.[82] Again, Alexander was acquitted. But the damage was done. Because of his unpopularity in Richmond, he was reassigned to a North Carolina prison. His glory days on the Richmond Theatre stage were over, too.

⟫·◦·⟪

After the war, Sallie Partington's talent took her to the stages of New York. In her later years, she would live in obscurity in Richmond, within seven short blocks of the scene of her wartime triumphs.[83] And while Alexander's name is forever synonymous with the dark horrors at Castle Thunder, Sallie Partington's 1907 obituary said, "Across the path of many a weary traveler she cast rays of sweet and inspiring sunshine."[84]

Immediately following the fall of Richmond, citizens wondered what became of Nero, Alexander's fierce, black dog. On May 1, 1865, less than a month after the city fell, the *Richmond Whig* ventured a guess. "We incline to the opinion," the paper said, "that his dogship evacuated with the rest of the Castle officials and joined Jeff. Davis to assist in the hunt after the Trans-Mississippi trail."[85]

Actually, Nero entered show business in New York City. In the summer of 1865, famous showman P.T. Barnum exhibited the dog at his American Museum on lower Broadway.[86] And, according to an 1895 issue of the *Richmond Times-Dispatch*, the "noble specimen of a Lordly Canine Race" even went on tour. Hyped with "flaming advertisements" and "grandiloquent" oratory, Nero was billed as "the dog which was kept at Libby Prison to eat Yankee prisoners." The public reveled in the show—a show that fattened many a Northern wallet.[87]

Chapter 8

CAMP LEE

Richmond's Chief Camp of Instruction

A stone's throw behind today's Science Museum of Virginia stood one of the very first Confederate training camps. A hub of fervent Southern patriotism, it molded tens of thousands of soldiers. It launched the careers of many officers, including a bearded man dubbed "Stonewall." And it was where Confederates executed the very first spy of the war.

The camp was less than a quarter mile back from Broad Street, and the intervening land was "rendered picturesque by a noble growth of oaks" and "rich pasturage." They were vestiges of a six-hundred-acre country estate owned by John Mayo Jr.—of Mayo Bridge fame. In 1789, he used his bridge fortune to build his country seat there, called the "Hermitage." It burned in 1857.

A year or two later, a sixty-three-acre portion of the estate was transformed into the Hermitage Fairgrounds, a venue for agricultural fairs. The Union Agricultural Fair of 1860, from October 22 to 27, drew tens of thousands to Richmond—a new record.[88] One newspaper trumpeted, "This vast assemblage, composed of the flower of our Virginia population—of our fair women and brave men—poured out day after day to the Fair grounds, excited by the bright skies and the beautiful and peaceful spectacle, and the interchanges of social courtesies and kindnesses, which none appreciate more highly than our Virginians."[89] The exhibits were impressive. "The horses, cattle, and other stock and articles exhibited, were admitted on all hands to be unusually fine," said one Virginia gentleman. "Intelligent foreigners remarked that the grounds were more beautiful than any they had seen in Europe."

Almost as soon as the Hermitage Fairground buildings were completed in late 1859 or early 1860, Governor Letcher was eyeing the site as a potential military training camp. John Brown's recent raid on Harpers Ferry convinced the governor of one thing—the state's defense trumped blue-ribbon Guernseys, goats and apple pies. Anxiety and dread were mounting by the week. "The land is now overshadowed with ominous clouds," said the *Dispatch* on October 31, 1860, "and none of us can tell how soon the services of the troops may be needed."[90] Much was riding on the outcome of the presidential election the following week.

Governor Letcher had a contingency plan. He organized a gathering of Virginia cavalry companies to take place just after the election at the Hermitage Fairgrounds. For the event, the site was named Camp Lee, after famed Revolutionary war cavalry officer "Light Horse Harry Lee."[91] No one knew it yet, but his son would soon be tapped for a major role in a new revolution.

Even as the polls opened on November 6, there were already rumblings in the South of resistance and disunion. Then, on the morning of November 8, the *Richmond Dispatch* ruefully declared Lincoln the victor. "The event is the most deplorable one that has happened in the history of the country," the paper proclaimed, adding that Virginia was "prepared to expect trouble."[92]

It was that same day that the cavalry event began. Providing Richmond a brilliant display of martial fervor, it whetted the city's appetite for war. With the Armory Band furnishing "excellent music," thirteen companies—with about forty members each—joined in dress parade.

To drill the troops, Governor Letcher invited a top military tactician, Colonel William J. Hardee. Between assignments with the U.S. Army, he would soon join the Confederacy. Hardee had recently put in a four-year stint at West Point as a tactics instructor and commandant of cadets. And back in 1855, at the behest of Secretary of War Jefferson Davis, Hardee published *Rifle and Light Infantry Tactics*—soon to become the best-known drill manual of the conflict. The troops now parading at Camp Lee passed before Hardee in review. He was impressed by the "magnificent spectacle" and the display of expert horsemanship.[93]

Later that afternoon, the troops were exercised in squad drill. Looking on was Governor Letcher himself, who for months had been busily securing arms for the state.

On the eve of war, U.S. Army colonel William J. Hardee came to Richmond to drill troops at Camp Lee. He went on to become a Confederate general, earning the nickname, "Old Reliable." *Library of Congress.*

The ladies of Richmond were anxious to see the excitement at Camp Lee for themselves. The next morning, under a threatening sky, they "assembled in throngs" at Richmond's railroad depot at Eighth and Broad Streets, "under the protection of their husbands, fathers, or beaux," and boarded the cars for the camp about two miles west. Meanwhile, the First Regiment formed on Capital Square with the band and drum corps and took up the line of march in the same direction. A great number of carriages loaded with passengers also departed for the camp, while other citizens set out on foot. By 11:30, *the seats overlooking the parade ground were crowded, and presented an array of bright colors that only wanted sunshine to make the picture more striking. A large number of ladies also occupied the verandah of the Exhibition Hall. The troops were manoevering [sic] on the area below, officers shouting the words of command, sabres clashing and plumes waving, while here and there a trooper, desirous of showing his skill in horsemanship, scampered off to some distant point as if he were entered for a four mile race. Everything wore a martial appearance, and everybody seemed to enjoy the spectacle.*

Drums sounded, announcing the arrival of the First Regiment from the city. The men entered the Broad Street gate, where they were met by a squadron of cavalry, and marched to the place of parade. The *Dispatch* raved, "The men marched well and exhibited in their general movements a proficiency showing their careful attention to the instructions of the drill-room." The spectators were equally impressed.

At noon, the review commenced. Governor Letcher rode on horseback through the lines, attended by Colonel Munford, secretary of the commonwealth; Colonel Hardee; and other officers. Later, as the entire body of troops marched around the field with pomp and circumstance, it began to rain. The spectators rushed for cover and departed, while the review went on.

After a dreadful, stormy night, the troops held exercises once more. In the early afternoon, commanding officer Colonel Sherwin McRae organized a parade to the city. The troops passed through Capitol Square and by the governor's mansion. Richmonders delighted in the splendid cavalcade. Then, late in the day, the troops packed up, "mounted their horses and bid adieu to Camp Lee."[94]

For five months, the fairgrounds lay quiet.

But everything changed on April 17, 1861, when Virginia seceded. Spirited volunteers from Virginia and beyond would soon stake out for Camp Lee to receive their first uniforms and weapons, get their regimental assignments and be trained for the bloody battles to come.

On Sunday, April 21, acting on Governor Letcher's orders, the VMI Corps of Cadets headed out to Richmond. Leading them was VMI professor Major Thomas J. Jackson—another rising star. Arriving at the Richmond train depot shortly after dark on the April 22—about the same moment that Robert E. Lee was sworn in as commander—the teenaged cadets marched to Capitol Square. After being reviewed by the governor, Jackson marched the cadets to Camp Lee.

Camp Lee took over the Hermitage Fairgrounds and swarmed with thousands of Confederate recruits. On the site today is the Science Museum of Virginia. *Library of Virginia.*

Jackson volunteered to serve as an artillery drillmaster at the camp, employing his cadets as drill instructors. Over the coming months, these 185 cadets would train 50,000 men in close-order drill and the manual of arms. But, as enthusiastic as Jackson was in this role, he itched for a field command. Just six days after he arrived in Richmond, Governor Letcher ordered him to take command at Harpers Ferry. Soon, Jackson would be heralded as the immortal "Stonewall" Jackson. After leaving for his new post, another VMI professor, Colonel William H. Gilham, was appointed first commandant of Camp Lee. He was the obvious choice. In 1860, in response to the raid on Harpers Ferry, he published a manual for training volunteers and militia, titled *Manual of Instruction for the Volunteers and Militia of the United States.*

On April 27, as volunteers poured into Richmond from all over the South, the *Enquirer* ran this notice from the Adjutant General's office:

> *VOLUNTEER COMPANIES, now in Richmond, or on their way to this point, will proceed at once to the Camp of Instruction, at the Hermitage Fair Grounds. The Captains will report in person to Lieut. CUNNINGHAM, Acting Assistant General.*[95]

Within a week of the cadets' arrival at Camp Lee, its population soared into the thousands. On April 29, about five thousand infantry troops were being trained at the camp, drilled five hours a day. Among the participating companies were the First Regiment of Virginia volunteers, the Lexington Cadets, the Hanover Grays, the Paineville Rifles, the Henrico Southern Guard, the Patrick Henry Rifles and the Ashland Grays. "Many of these companies are well drilled and perfectly efficient," the *Enquirer* said. Laying it on thick, the paper added, "Some of them seem as if a bullet would have little effect in stopping them, if once ordered to 'charge.'" The *Dispatch* reported that "the best spirit prevails among the men."[96]

Many of the soldiers wrote home from Camp Lee, providing a window into camp life. On April 28, 1861, Andrew C.L. Gatewood wrote:

My Dear Parents

I was surprised yesterday evening when I met Mr. Skeen, and he told me that you all did not know where I was. He said you thought I was at Harpers Ferry & when you found out that I was not at Harpers F. you still thought that I was in Lexington. I wrote you three letters a few days...before we left Lexington telling you that we would leave on Monday, but the news came sooner than I expected. We were ordered off at nine o'clock on Sunday this day week, but we did not expect to leave before Monday therefore we were not ready. But we got ready and left at 1 o'clock on Sunday. We rode to Staunton on stages, wagons, hacks, and all kinds of vehicles. We got to Staunton at 4 o'clock Monday morning. We left Staunton at 9 o'clock arrived at Richmond on Tuesday morning at 3 o'clock, since then we have been busily engaged in drilling recruits for the Army. There are now 3,000 troops on the Fair Grounds.

I suppose you heard that Major Gilham has been promoted to Colonel, Major Jackson to Colonel, Lt. S. Ship Asst. Adjt General. We are engaged every day drilling squads. The cadets have the best name now of any Corps in the U. States. The people say they keep them selves so clean and nice and drill so well, we have gained a high reputation since we came to R'd.

You must excuse me for bad writing as I am in a hurry, & have a bad pen, also not well fixed to write...We can't go to R. but once a month. Give my love to sister Mary & Will, also to Mr. Coffee, Bonner. Tell Mr. Stofer I want get him down here in my squad to double quick him some. I know I can run him to death without getting tired my self. Please send me some money. I want to buy some clothes that I need very badly…Give my love to all.

Good bye
Your son
A.C.L. Gatewood

Serving as Camp Lee's hospital were the new fairground exhibition hall and horticultural hall,[97] which tended sick soldiers almost from the start. Local newspapers made appeals for help. "Our lady friends may add materially to the comfort of the sick soldiers now in hospital at the Camp of Instruction," said the *Dispatch* on April 30, "by sending them baked custards, eggs, milk, etc."[98] Over the course of the war, there were between five hundred to fifteen thousand patients there at any given time. Diseases were rampant, as with all the camps.

The commandant's headquarters were in a remote building, which during agricultural fairs was called the "President's Office." A long building beyond the headquarters was occupied by quartermasters, surgeons and drill masters. In front of that was an enclosed space where the officers sought evening recreation "playing games with marbles." And scattered across the grounds were white tents for the enlisted men.[99]

In those first heady weeks of secession, crowds of Richmond ladies and gentlemen visited Camp Lee at sundown to watch the battalion drills and dress parades. "The proficiency of the Lexington Cadets" was "something wonderful to behold," said the *Richmond Whig* on May 22, "and worth going a long distance to see."[100]

Volunteering as chaplain at the camp was Reverend Moses D. Hoge of Richmond's Second Presbyterian church. Devoted to the "spiritual good of the soldier," he delivered eloquent sermons at the parade grounds. Many men were deeply moved. According to Reverend Hoge, some of the newly enlisted regiments were there for a few weeks, and others for several months, "as the exigencies of the case might demand." He claimed to have seen one hundred thousand men pass through the camp during his connection with it.[101]

Shortly after dawn on May 29, newly elected Confederate president Jefferson Davis arrived by train in Richmond. After being greeted with wild cheers and a salute of fifteen guns, he made a speech at the Spotswood Hotel. Then, in the early evening, he proceeded to Camp Lee, "accompanied by a cortege on horseback" to review the troops. There, "a large number of ladies and gentlemen had assembled, and on his arrival greeted him with the heartiest demonstrations of pleasure." Davis dismounted his horse and shook hands with the enthusiastic crowd. In a short speech, he told the volunteers they were "the last best hope of liberty." A local paper gushed, "The Commander-in-Chief was pleased with his men—they with him."[102]

Around this same period, a new recruit arrived at the camp, giving Reverend Hoge a rush of pride and patriotism. It was his nephew, Edgar Marquess. Reverend Hoge wrote his sister, Ann:

My Dear Sister: I do not know how I can gratify you more than to write you something about your "bold soldier boy."

I saw him mustered into service by the inspector-general on the arrival of the company in Richmond, and I was present when they marched into the "Camp of Instruction," where they are now quartered in their pretty white tents. Edgar is the most soldierly looking man in the company—erect, tall and martial in his bearing...At night I preached in camp, where I have voluntarily been acting as chaplain for about five weeks, and preaching as often as my other engagements would permit. I did not ask such an appointment, but, without my solicitation, the Military Bureau last week gave me a commission as chaplain. I hope I shall be stationed at the "Camp of Instruction" about two miles from the city, and then I shall not be separated from my congregation.

...With my whole mind and heart I go into the secession movement. I think providence has devolved on us the preservation of constitutional liberty, which has already been trampled under the foot of a military despotism at the North. And now that we are menaced with subjugation for daring to assert the right of self-government, I consider our contest as one which involves principles more important than those for which our fathers of the Revolution contended.

...You may rest assured that Edgar shall have all the care and attention we can give him during his stay in camp. It will give me great pleasure to serve him in any way.

I have fitted up a large tent at the camp and provided it with a fine library of books and magazines, as a free reading-room for the men. It will afford much pleasure particularly to the Hampden-Sidney boys.

Oddly enough, some of the volunteers arriving at Camp Lee didn't speak English. In June 1861, Creoles from Louisiana were drilled in French by Prince de Polignac of France, who'd just offered his services to the

Confederacy. Country boys from backwoods Georgia listened with their mouths agape.[103] Days later, Polignac began his distinguished war career in earnest as lieutenant colonel of infantry under General P.G.T. Beauregard. Eventually, Polignac would become a major general.

The war was in full swing by July 1861 with the bloody battle at Manassas. The heat was on for the cadets at Camp Lee to churn out trained soldiers. That same month, General Lee appointed Colonel Charles Dimmock as Camp Lee's new commandant.

That December, Dimmock was replaced by Colonel John C. Shields—who would eventually have a lake named in his honor at Richmond's Byrd Park. As Shields took command, Camp Lee was designated Richmond's camp for artillery instruction, and the infantry were scattered elsewhere.

———————

In April 1862, with the spring campaigns looming, Camp Lee was the site of a highly publicized execution. A man named Timothy Webster had recently been arrested in Richmond as a Union spy. The evidence was undeniable. Posing as a Southern gentleman, he was a detective with the Pinkerton Agency, gathering information on the Confederacy and sending reports to Washington. Webster was convicted by court martial. On the morning of April 29, provost marshal George W. Alexander took him from Castle Godwin Prison to Camp Lee to be hanged. When brought to the gallows, just erected under a clump of old oak trees, "the prisoner was visibly affected by the sight of the preparations observable, and shuddered when he looked at his coffin."[104] The rope was adjusted around his neck, prayer was offered by Reverend Hoge and a black cap was drawn over Webster's eyes. The signal was given. The noose slipped, and he fell on his back to the ground. As his captors re-rigged the rope, Webster said, "I suffer a double death!" The second attempt was successful, and the body hung for a half hour before being cut down. Timothy Webster was the first spy to be executed in the war.

From that day forward, Camp Lee was designated the site for executing spies and deserters—the latter by firing squad. Crowds of the morbidly curious turned out to witness the events. Camp Lee was also the post at which the paroled and exchanged Confederate soldiers were sent from northern prisons. There they drew pay, clothing and subsistence until they could be exchanged and returned to their command in the field.

That same April, the first Confederate Conscription Act was passed. That heaped more duties on Camp Lee's commandant, Colonel Shields. He was also made commandant of conscripts for Virginia—with headquarters at Camp Lee for that purpose.

Suddenly, a different breed of men began pouring into Camp Lee—ones there against their will. Discipline became a major problem. Fighting, smashing windows, breaking furniture and other rowdy behavior were everyday occurrences. Desertion was another issue. Interestingly, among the many conscripts who eventually escaped were four men from the "Iron Clad Opera Troupe," which had performed at Metropolitan Hall in Richmond.[105]

In May came the Battle of Seven Pines, followed by the Seven Days' Battles in June and July. By necessity, men at the various camps of instruction were often rushed off to battle before they were fully trained.

On May 2, 1863, "Stonewall" Jackson was shot by friendly fire. Eight days later, he died. The South deeply mourned its beloved hero. On May 12, the elaborate military funeral procession ambled through the streets of Richmond, culminating at the Capitol. There, he lay in state, and a large crowd lined up to pay their respects. Ladies kissed his coffin. The "Napoleon of the South"—who'd begun his brilliant Civil War career at Camp Lee—was gone forever.

Conscripts continued pouring into Camp Lee. In October 1863, Governor Letcher reported that "upwards of thirty thousand" of them had passed through the camp.[106]

As the war grinded on through 1864, Camp Lee certainly shared in the misfortunes of the Confederacy—with shortages of rations, supplies and manpower. By January 1865, the picturesqueness of the fairgrounds was long gone. The whole place was tattered and worn—emblematic of the Confederates' sinking hopes.

Then, on April 3, 1865, the Union troops finally marched victorious into the Confederate Capital, while a raging fire consumed the city's core. The Twenty-eighth U.S. Colored Troops marched in formation west on Broad Street. Gleefully, newly freed slaves rushed in to touch their liberators. The massive throng followed until the troops reached Camp Lee. Union soldiers shook hands with the grateful former slaves.

Amidst the revelry at Camp Lee, a miracle occurred for the regiment's chaplain, Reverend Garland White. Born into slavery in nearby Hanover County, he was separated from his mother during his boyhood and sold to Georgia congressman Robert Toombs. Later, he escaped and fled north. Now, as he thrilled to "the shouts of ten thousand voices" celebrating liberation in the former Confederate Capital, an old woman approached him. She asked his name, his birthplace and the name of his mother. After he answered all of her questions, she said, "This is your mother, Garland, whom you are now talking to, who has spent twenty years of grief about her son."

A huge mass of Union troops made their headquarters there at Camp Lee, including the Fourth Massachusetts Cavalry—arguably the first troops to enter the city and work to extinguish the fire.[107]

On April 4, the day after Richmond fell, President Lincoln arrived in the city and surveyed the burned-out city. After a stop at the Confederate White House, he was driven by carriage to Camp Lee and then to Capitol Square.[108]

By the following month, twenty cabins located about three hundred yards from the Camp Lee hospital were occupied by about two hundred newly emancipated slaves. The Union soldiers called the community Gorée, after an island off the coast of Senegal, Africa.

By that fall, the Camp Lee site was occupied by the Freedmen's Bureau. It included a "negro orphan asylum" and a school for children of all ages. In the following year, "thirty to forty tenements" at the camp housed "three to five hundred negroes" at any given time.[109] Ironically, this site—for four years complicit in perpetuating slavery—was now dedicated to helping blacks.

In April 1867, the Camp Lee site witnessed another transformation. It became the Hermitage Trotting Park, with a circular, half-mile horse track and a beer garden. A few racehorses gave the hallowed place a lively, new reputation, including Grey Sam, Fanny Baker and Katie Darling.[110]

Chapter 9

The Mordecai Ladies

Emotions Run High at "Rosewood"

Full of excitement, fifty-one-year-old spinster Emma Mordecai arrived at the modest farmhouse on the knoll, called, "Rosewood." It was April 18, 1864, and the trees were just leafing out. Since Emma's mother had died six months earlier in Richmond, this was a new beginning—even if it was wartime.

Emma's sister-in-law, Rosina—nicknamed "Rose"—welcomed her to Rosewood for an extended stay. "Rose had prepared most kindly for my reception," Emma wrote, "and my room was the picture of neatness & comfort." The 279-acre farm was worked by slaves, growing wheat and vegetables to sustain the household and sell at market. A cow grazed with her calf on the grassy slopes, providing milk and butter. Beyond the little green hills to the north was a shimmering millpond, called "Young's Pond." The wheat was ground into flour in the mill house. The Rosewood house had a separate kitchen. There were also two icehouses, a smokehouse, a chicken house, a hog pen and a dairy barn.

Three times during the war, Confederates converged on the farm. In the early days of the conflict, General W.H.F. "Rooney" Lee used Rosewood as his headquarters. In June 1862, J.E.B. Stuart "quietly concentrated" 1,200 of his men on the farm. And the Georgia Infantry made their winter quarters in the pine woods behind the house.[111]

Located five miles northwest of Richmond in today's Bryan Park, the Rosewood house was noticeably absent of men. Rose was widowed, and

Rosewood, the Mordecai home. The family farm became Bryan Park in 1910. *Valentine Richmond History Center.*

her three sons—John, George and William—were serving in the Richmond Howitzers artillery. Still at Rose's knee was her sixteen-year-old daughter, Augusta—nicknamed "Gusta"—who was attending school in the city.

Rose's brother, attorney John Brooke Young, lived at the adjoining farm to the east, called "Westbrook." He and Rose had grown up on the farm, where today is the Westminster Canterbury retirement village.

Emma grew up at nearby Spring Farm, the site of today's Lakeside neighborhood. Rose eventually married Emma's brother Augustus Mordecai, who died in the 1840s. Since Rose and Emma had grown up together, their ties ran deep.

Rose was lucky to have so much family support at this critical time. Not only was she worried sick about her sons in battle, but Rosewood itself lay prone to enemy attack from the north. The farm lay just inside Richmond's Outer Defenses, with small artillery fortifications carved into the hillsides along incoming roads.

To make matters even grimmer for Rose, she was barely making ends meet. "Rose is & has always been one of the rich poor people—such a good economist," Emma wrote.

Emma had started a diary on her first day at Rosewood, providing a vivid record of the tumultuous, final year of the war. A longtime resident of Richmond, she was already toughened by the conflict. But her mettle would soon be tested, as the horrors of war pierced the pastoral serenity of Rosewood.

⸻⸱◦⸱⸻

As much as the Mordecai ladies were devoted to the Confederate cause and followed the war news, they tried to go about their normal daily activities—like sewing, knitting, writing letters and receiving visitors. Gusta also practiced playing the piano. During the first week of Emma's stay, Rose was helping alter Gusta's summer dresses, since they couldn't afford new ones. "No young girl in the Confederacy will be more prettily or amply supplied with an outfit for the summer," Emma wrote.

On the pleasant spring evening of May 5, Emma and Gusta headed out on foot to Westbrook, where they'd been invited for supper and family togetherness. They could see campfires up in the woods near Brook Turnpike, and General Pickett's wagons were "moving up the turnpike to the new camp" close to Westbrook. Soldiers swarmed to Westbrook's well to fill their canteens.

The Youngs served a fine supper "that would have done credit to the most abundant times." Afterward, they all gathered around for some "sweet music." With Gusta at the piano, Mrs. Young sang some of her favorite songs. Then, shouts rang out from the new camp. The men had been ordered right back to Chaffin's Farm, the place they'd just left, since "the Yankees were said to be coming up James River in transports & gunboats." Mrs. Young was visibly shaken by the news. When her brother, Dr. Braxton, laughed at her, she explained she was "full of fear."

"Well, that is a very good thing to fill up with, in these scarce times," he quipped.

Emma was about to get her first taste of fear at Rosewood. On May 10, she and Rose heard heavy firing from the south. "The servants say they have heard it when at work in the field, all the morning," Emma scribbled in her diary. "The enemy seem to be making an attack on all sides."

Emma found strength through her staunch Jewish faith. "I still feel undismayed," she declared, "& pray God to enable us to endure whatever awaits us in the way of evil, with fortitude, and to receive with humble gratitude what may await us in the way of success."

Just hours later, Mr. Young brought the ladies urgent news from Westbrook. The Yankees were approaching Richmond from the north, so they should quickly hide all their valuables. Rose had slaves take down the meat in the smokehouse. Emma hid a few of her keepsakes, then went right back to making a dress. "We were aware that at any moment the Philistines might be upon us," she wrote, likening the Yankees to the invaders of ancient Israel, "but we went on quietly with our occupations."

The next morning, Emma and Rose worked in the strawberry patch with slave girls Lizzy, Mary and Georgiana. Suddenly, male slaves Cyrus and George ran up with an urgent update from Westbrook. Yankees were in force just three miles north. Mr. Young had warned the slaves to be on the lookout, and be ready to hide the horse and mule in the woods. Unbeknownst to all of them, Union General Sheridan was conducting a raid on Richmond. That afternoon, General J.E.B. Stuart tried to fight off the Yankees at Yellow Tavern on Brook Turnpike. The battle was lost, with Stuart wounded in the belly and rushed to Richmond for care.

Violent storms arrived that evening—enough to blow the steeple and bell tower off of St. John's Church in the Church Hill neighborhood.[112]

At first light the next morning, May 12, the Mordecai ladies heard "heavy cannonading and rounds of musketry somewhere to the east." It raged for an hour or two. Slave George, who had stayed at Westbrook the previous night, reported that "a number of Yankees were over there all night & that the turnpike is full of them." That spelled serious trouble. The Yankees had breached the city's Outer Defenses. At about 8:00 that morning, Emma frightfully wrote, "Another thunderstorm is answering the booming of the cannon & the crack of the musketry, which continue but at longer intervals. We know nothing but that fighting is going on all around us, & that our pickets have been withdrawn to the inner lines of defences, which leaves us in the enemy's lines."

The Mordecai ladies were in mortal fear. A fierce battle was being waged about a mile east of Brook Turnpike on the Military Road, today's Azalea Avenue. The battle would be dubbed "The Brook Church Fight," after a church then situated at the corner of Brook Turnpike and Military Road. The fighting didn't end until about 4:00 that afternoon.[113]

As soon as the rain let up, Emma and Rose cautiously ventured out to see what happened. They walked to the entrance of the Westbrook lane, where county pickets were stationed. One of the men claimed that the Confederates had had "a small force, not more than 600 to oppose a large number of Yankees."

Shortly after the ladies returned home to Rosewood, a neighbor dropped by with "joyful tidings" about the recent contest. The Confederates had driven the Yankees off, he said, and they were now beyond the Chickahominy, with Fitz Lee still after them. Emma's heart "swelled with gratitude for this signal deliverance." But there was bad news to go with the good. That morning, their brave General J.E.B. Stuart had died in Richmond.

Slaves brought news of the wounded. Some had been taken to Brook Church and other places on Brook Turnpike, while others had been taken by ambulance to Richmond. "What a cruel, frightful mystery is War!" Emma wailed with her pen.

Right after breakfast the next morning, Emma and Rose decided to go up to Brook Turnpike and see if they could assist any wounded still in the area. After Rose packed up some biscuits and filled some jugs with milk and buttermilk, they headed out by carriage. As soon as they reached Brook Turnpike, it was obvious that all the wounded had been sent to the city. Then, Emma suggested

> that we should visit part of the scene of yesterday's encounter, only a mile beyond the turnpike, but we found many difficulties to our progress, trees felled across the roads, dead horses—and finally were frightened by seeing a body of cavalry moving some distance ahead of us, whom we feared might be Yankees, so we turned from our attempt. We saw some large trees topped by cannon balls, & others badly cut by them, & a good many people in the woods looking for plunder—but except these, and the dead horses & the badly cut up roads, we saw no evidences of the hard fight which took place there only yesterday.

Emma and Rose drove on to Richmond, delivering the milk and biscuits to the Officers' Hospital. They also checked on relatives in the city.

That night back at Rosewood, they received an encouraging word. "There had been no casualties among the Richmond Howitzers to which our three boys, William, John & George Mordecai belong," Emma cheerfully wrote.

The next day, with heavy, constant firing heard from the south, the Mordecai ladies received a note from sixteen-year-old Belle Stewart of

Brook Hill, "giving tidings of the safety of [the Mordecai] boys." It said that, two days earlier, "Genl. Lee had gained a great victory." But Rose refused to put any faith in the news whatsoever. Emma snapped, telling Rose "she hugged worry with the closest affection." For the rest of the evening, Rose gave Emma the silent treatment, and Emma went to bed feeling miserable.

The next morning, Emma went to Rose, saying she was "very sorry to have made that disagreeable remark…last night, to which [Rose] replied, she had given me as sharp an answer, & that she was sorry too." Offering an olive branch, Emma accompanied Rose to Christian services at Emmanuel Episcopal on Brook Turnpike.

<hr />

More tragic news descended on Rosewood a few days later. Rose learned that her cousin, Lawrence Young, had been badly wounded and taken to a makeshift hospital in Seabrook's warehouse. She swiftly departed for Richmond with a neighbor to check on him.

When she got back that evening, she gave a full report. She'd "found her poor cousin, with his leg amputated above the knee, lying amidst crowds of sufferers in the same or worse condition." Rose and her neighbor "had been busy from the time they got to the Hospital, trying to do what they could for the poor sufferers." A steady stream of wounded had been brought in, and the bare-armed surgeons did "their dreadful work" in the yard of the building.

Emma was deeply moved. Brave and noble men were "now more prostrate & helpless than infants," and the hospitals desperately needed assistance. The very next morning, she took the train into the city to "alleviate their sufferings," carrying "buttermilk, sweetmilk & some other things." She tended as many injured men as she could. That evening, with her typical patriotic fervor, she wrote, "All that can be said or sung of brave deeds done, & their consequent sufferings borne with noble heroism, would fail to do justice to our southern heroes."

After just one day providing care at the hospitals, Emma found her calling. For the rest of the war, she would continue tending the "pure high-minded, noble men"—many of them bloodied amputees. One evening, after returning to Rosewood, she recorded in her diary, "Ladies untiring, men very grateful; say they cannot fight hard enough for such ladies."

The most harrowing week imaginable for the Mordecai ladies began on Sunday, April 2, 1865. Shortly before sunset, "like the crash of a terrific thunder-bolt," they learned that the Yankees were closing in on Richmond, and the city was to be evacuated by midnight. "Language has no power to describe the dismay, the grief and the appalling terror, produced by such tidings," Emma wrote. "My heart ached for all my friends in the City, for our boys in the field whom we knew to be suffering intense anxiety if indeed, they were yet alive to suffer anything."

Just before dawn the next morning, a terrific explosion shook the house to its foundation. Emma bolted up in bed horror-stricken, groped her way downstairs and got into bed with Rose and Gusta. They huddled together, all atremble. Then came even more explosions.

Everything finally fell quiet. Rose decided Gusta should be rushed to the city to be with friends. Rose was also anxious to retrieve some valuable old silver pieces from the bank, before all the stores got sacked. She quickly arranged for slave George to take Emma and Gusta to the city by mule-drawn cart. The ladies didn't know it yet, but the explosions had originated from Richmond itself. The city's powder magazine and arsenal had been blown up—along with gunboats in the James River—so that nothing of value would fall into Yankee hands. To top it all off, much of the city's core was on fire.

In the bright light of morning, Emma and Gusta climbed into the cart, and George drove them off. Along the road, they passed soldiers hurrying away from the city. "You are going to a bad place," one of them warned. Continuing on, Emma and Gusta noticed plumes of smoke rising in the distance from Richmond. As they neared the city, they heard a devastating report—enemy troops had marched into the Confederate Capital. Terrified, Gusta was "crazy to return to her mother," so George halted the mule and the ladies got out of the cart. But George continued onward. He'd heard the Confederate officials were handing out flour and meat, since the city was being abandoned anyway.

As Emma and Gusta fled back home, they were cowered by "the incessant roar of one explosion after another, or of many together, [which] were multiplied by the repeated reverberations from hill to hill, in terrible grandeur."

They were greatly relieved when they reached the relative safety of Rosewood. Gusta rushed into her mother's arms. Then, Rose "lay down and read a number of appropriate Psalms & hymns," while Gusta and Emma nervously busied themselves knitting. After nightfall, the noises from the city finally ceased.

The next morning, April 5, Rose's brother came by with horrible news: fire had destroyed much of Richmond. The ladies couldn't imagine things getting any worse.

Then, shortly after Rose's brother left, they heard horse hooves in the yard. Cautiously, Emma went to the door. "There, close by the porch, on a bare-backed horse, sat an insolent looking negro, dirty and ragged." It was an officer with the U.S. Colored Troops, saying he had orders "to take ev'y horse & saddle outside de lines." Suddenly, the ladies realized he was mounted on Rose's only horse.

"Now I want de saddle, so han' it out, and be quick 'bout it," the officer bellowed. Reluctantly, Rose had slave girl Mary bring the saddle out, and the officer threw it over the horse's back. Rose inched out into the yard to admonish the officer, but when he saw her coming he galloped away.

Emma fumed. She was convinced the man had no authority for his conduct. Determined to get the horse and saddle back, she defiantly marched toward Camp Lee near town to "see what could be done." Rather than going alone, she took slave girls Mary and Georgiana—and "committed [her] undertaking to God."

When the threesome reached Camp Lee, Emma saw that the Confederates were gone, and the place had turned "black and blue with well equipped negro troops." She was directed to General Alonzo G. Draper, "a sleek, dapper, unmilitary looking man," who told her she'd have to take up her issue with another command elsewhere. On top of facing this impossible task, Emma was told she couldn't return home without a pass from the provost marshal in the city.

Emma and the slave girls walked the two or three miles along Broad Street into Richmond. Exhausted, Emma found her city almost unrecognizable. "Everything looked full of rubbish and disorder bespeaking ruin," she agonized. As she neared Sixth Street, the sidewalks were covered with broken glass from the storefront windows, "reduced to powder from the explosions." Emancipated slaves were celebrating boisterously.

Turning right onto Ninth Street, Emma found one block "ankle deep with fragments of Confederate printed blanks & other papers." The Capital grounds were "filthy" and "thronged with a motley crowd of a native & foreign negroes." As mounted Yankee officers galloped up to the Capital steps, citizens were filing in and out of the provost marshal's office, looking "disconsolate, desolate and defiled." Emma went inside and got a pass to return home to Rosewood.

Hoping to find slave George, she ambled through the burnt district, "a scene of desolation and destruction." When she heard that enemy leader Abraham Lincoln had arrived in town via the James River, she quipped, "Then it is time for me to go out." Just as she turned, she spotted George watering his mule. Scampering to him, she got in the cart along with the slave children. George was tipsy, having done a little celebrating of his own.

As George clumsily drove the group to the city's edge, they passed an "insolent" picket who Emma described as "a Black ruffian." Under her breath, she cursed his race and Lincoln, too, as "ill-bred." The man pointed his musket at her. "You haven't got things here no longer as you have had them," he snapped. "Don't you know that? Don't you know that?"

Emma and the others managed to get back home just after dark, much to the relief of Rose and Gusta. Emma told them about a kind Yankee who'd escorted her part of the way to town. He'd assured her "that no interruption to property...would be permitted, and that the discipline was very strict." It seemed Rose might get her horse back after all. Finally, the Mordecai ladies spent a peaceful night.

The next day, Emma was surprised to find Cyrus "sitting idle" under a hedge. He told her that "there was to be no more Master & Mistress now, all was equal"—he "done hear dat read from the Court House Steps." Regardless, he intended to keep living at Rosewood. "All the land belongs to the Yankees now," he claimed, "they gwine divide it out 'mong de coloured people. Besides, de kitchen ob de big house is my share. I help built it."

On April 9, the Mordecai ladies heard volleys of artillery all night long. They later learned it was fired by Yankees, celebrating General Lee's surrender. "This was agony piled on agony," Emma wrote. "Rose sat on the floor before the fire, weeping bitterly. Gusta was dissolved in tears, and felt as if every ray of joy had departed from her young life."

As for Emma, she felt "utterly miserable," wishing that "the earth might open & swallow us all up."

<hr>

On the afternoon of April 16, the ladies heard footsteps approaching the house. Their fears mounted, suspecting it was Yankees again. *But it was their precious boys, John and George, returning home from war.*

As the door flung open, Rose was overcome with joy and emotion. She didn't think she'd ever see them again, yet here they were, safe and sound. "What a wonderful mercy!" Emma wrote in her diary. "They had walked thirty miles yesterday. They are wonderfully cheerful, but like Genl. Lee they have the comfort of knowing they have done their whole duty as brave constant soldiers."

The boys said their brother William was on his way with a mule he had been allowed to bring out with him. "So they are all unhurt after such dangers, and exposure—privation & fatigue and hardships," Emma wrote, "as God's mercy & protection alone could have preserved them through." The boys were grateful for the enemy's conduct to them after the surrender—they said General Grant had even "refused to take Lee's sword."

William showed up at Rosewood early the next morning. Sharing a happy reunion, the whole family sat in the chamber and talked for hours. "Much of the greatest interest, to hear & to tell on both sides," Emma enthused.

The boys had no time for rest, however, going right to work on the farm.

———»·◊·«———

In early May, without warning, slave Cyrus began packing up to leave Rosewood. He'd rented a house near Brook Turnpike and told Rose he was taking his entire family with him, including his wife, Sarah, and daughter, Lizzy. He was also taking his slave daughters at Westbrook, Martha and Caroline.

Rose was very upset to see her slaves go—especially Cyrus. She confided to Emma, "If they felt as I do, they could not possibly leave me." But nothing could stop them. Rose gave them all "presents of old dresses &c. and also some meat, meal & potatoes, for all of which they seemed very grateful."

Finally, all of the former slaves departed for good, leaving the Mordecai family without a single servant. Rose quickly lapsed into a depression.

The next day, Emma bemoaned the agonizing, chaotic state of affairs in the South: "What an uprooting of social ties, and tearing asunder of almost kindred associations, and destruction of true loyalty, this strange, new, state of things produced!! The disturbance to the Whites & the privations it will at first entail upon the poor, improvident negroes, is incalculable."

That afternoon, feeling quite depressed, Emma wandered over to Westbrook. There, out on Brook Turnpike, was a disheartening display:

Several Corps of Grant's Army had been passing up the turnpike all day—returning to Washington, there to be disbanded. I went on top of the house to see the living stream, in one compact mass pouring up the road as far as the eye could reach in both directions. An admirably disciplined and well organized force—No straggling—no uproar—a quiet, steady stream—moving in an almost unbroken current. They have finished their work of destruction and subjugation…ruining a few more farms in their progress.

As the column of Yankee troops marched over the horizon near Brook Hill, "in triumph to uninjured, undisturbed homes & customs," the future seemed bleak indeed for the Mordecai ladies. The city of Richmond was ruined, physically and economically. Rose was hopelessly depressed because the South had lost the war and because her slaves—for whom she had deep feelings—were gone forever. Gusta was very sad too, having said goodbye to the Stewart daughters of Brook Hill, who'd escaped to Europe with their family.

And then there was Emma. The last words in her war diary, dated May 26, 1865, were: "I can only seem to observe nothing, and to feel nothing."

Chapter 10

COPING WITHOUT COFFEE

Coffee Substitute Factory Meets Violent End

A refined young lady named Sarah D. Eggleston, who grew up on her father's plantation, was seated primly and properly in a Norfolk hotel. Taking a sip of her coffee, she nearly gagged. Turns out, it was a coffee substitute, or "Confederate coffee"—in this case, made of parched meal. "Not only was it the first I ever tasted but the last," Sarah remarked, "for after that I took cold water in preference to any and all counterfeits of coffee."[114] Her gastronomic mishap took place during the winter of 1861–62, while similar scenes played out all across the Confederacy. Real coffee was scarce because of the Union blockade of ports and unprecedented global demand. Any coffee to be had in Dixie was priced through the proverbial roof.

Still, Southerners had a habit to maintain. Looking hard and fast for the perfect substitute, they developed numerous concoctions. Dry samples were sent to many newspaper editors. The *Richmond Dispatch* claimed you would "thank them for a good cup of coffee" if you mixed five parts parched red wheat with one part parched coffee, added a little butter or egg white and brewed the mixture in an "Old Dominion" coffeepot.[115] An editor from the *Natchez Daily Courier* in Mississippi claimed to have tasted a "very palatable" brew made from cotton seeds, parched and ground. It even had a coffee-like aroma. To ensure passing the taste test, however, he suggested "a mixture of one-third or one-half Coffee, and the rest of ground or powdered Cotton Seed."[116]

Coffee lovers suffered another devastating blow in the spring of 1862. The Federals captured New Orleans and some of the Atlantic seaports, choking off the coffee supply even further. That November, the *Savannah Republican* offered an elaborate, new recipe in its column, "Practical Hints for Hard Times." Coffee could be "perfectly counterfeited" in taste, they claimed, when combining these ingredients in equal parts: "Rye, wheat, barley (scalded and then parched,) okra seed, rice (parched black, but not ground,) sweet potatoes (cut into ribbons, or into dice, dried in the sun and then parched,) corn grits (parched to a dark brown,) sweet acorns, and chicory (parched brown, then broken and ground.)"

They assured if you added in a little coffee, "The best critic can scarcely distinguish between the spurious compound" and the real thing.[117]

All across the South, newspapers swore by everything from parched persimmon seeds to carrots, parsnips and beets. "In fact, all that is wanted is something to color the water," quipped a Georgia editor, "and you can fancy and call the concoction what you please. It is coffee or it is dirty water just as you please to imagine."[118]

In the fall of 1863, an editor with the *Montgomery Weekly Advertiser* claimed he'd tasted a brew "as good as the best." It was made with okra seeds, ground and parched. He claimed if the seeds were parched slowly and carefully without burning them, they would yield "as good a cup of coffee as anybody but a Confederate quartermaster, a successful blockade runner, or a sugar speculator can afford to drink."[119]

Richmond businessman David Baker Jr. marketed his own unique blend of Confederate coffee. It was famous. The factory was in a large brick building on Cary Street between Seventeenth and Eighteenth Streets. In the immediate vicinity were three notorious military prisons: Libby, Castle Thunder and Castle Lightning. Baker's factory had furnaces for parching and machines for grinding. His formula consisted of parched peas and corn, ground together. Advertised as "'Confederate Mills' Fresh Ground Coffee, an excellent substitute for the pure article," it sold for twenty cents per "neatly labeled" pound.[120]

In February 1864, just days before the Dahlgren-Kilpatrick Raid, even this substitute coffee supply dried up. Shortly after midnight on February 23, the factory caught fire. The clerk of the establishment was asleep when the fire broke out and barely escaped with his life.[121] The *Richmond Sentinel* gave a riveting account of the fateful blaze:

> *During the progress of the fire a very large steam boiler, in which had been left a supply of water, became red hot, and owing to the pressure of the steam engendered thereby a terrible explosion took place. The force of the*

explosion was so great that pieces of the boiler were driven through heavy brick walls, and large portions of it were thrown from a hundred to a hundred and fifty yards from the place at which it was stationed. One piece, weighing between three and four hundred pounds, was lodged in the prison yard at Castle Thunder, a square off, and fell within a few inches of one of the guard, the force of which so stunning him as to knock him senseless for a few minutes. A tenement in Hughes's row, on 17th street, was also struck by a piece of iron and a hole driven entirely through it.

The explosion was so forceful, added the *Sentinel,* that a young man in the area was struck in the head by a "flake" of the boiler and died soon thereafter.[122]

As the fire raged, military prisoners in the area were terrified that the blaze would spread and burn them alive. Luckily, they were spared. "The Fire Brigade were promptly on the spot," reported the *Dispatch,* "and did valuable service in saving from destruction the surrounding buildings."[123] While the prisons were merely scorched, the Confederate coffee factory was completely destroyed. Baker's loss was upwards of $60,000 in machinery and supplies.

The wealthy owner of the building, Franklin Stearns of Tree Hill Farm, suffered a loss of about $100,000. A whiskey distiller of Northern birth, he owned a large amount of real estate throughout the city. Two years earlier, right after martial law was declared in the city, he was suspected of being a Unionist. Confederates charged that his house was "a rendezvous for Lincoln sympathizers"[124] and threw him in Castle Godwin prison—located in a warehouse he himself owned. Following a court martial the following month, he was "entirely exonerated."[125]

The fire at the Confederate coffee factory was attributed to the drying furnaces, since they ran throughout the night. Describing the destruction after the blaze, the *Sentinel* added a word of warning: "A portion of the walls alone remain standing, and is liable to fall at any moment—the curious had, therefore, better be careful in the approach."[126]

Real coffee finally began flowing freely in the South the next year. But it came at the highest price ever—the loss of the Confederate cause.

Chapter 11

BORN FIGHTER, MARY EDWARDS WALKER

Union Doctor Imprisoned at the Castle

O n April 21, 1864, Confederates marched their newest political prisoner through the streets of Richmond, bound for Castle Thunder Prison. But this was no ordinary prisoner of war. It was the petite, thirty-one-year-old field surgeon and feminist Dr. Mary Edwards Walker, in a shocking get-up. The *Richmond Whig* reported on the scene:

> *She was dressed in male costume—black pants, fitting tight, a jacket and short talma of black or dark blue cloth, but wore a dark straw Gipsy hat, that might be construed as announcing her sex. She gave her name as Dr. Mary E. Walker, of the Union army, and said she was a regular allopathic physician. She said also that she had been improperly taken prisoner, as at the time of her capture she was on neutral ground. As she passed through the streets in charge of a detective, her unique appearance attracted unusual attention, and an immense crowd of negroes and idlers formed for her a volunteer escort to Castle Thunder.*[127]

It was Dr. Walker's trousers that stood out like a sore thumb. At the time, "real women" wore corsets and hoop skirts.

No shrinking violet, Dr. Walker was accustomed to bucking tradition. She'd been working in a man's profession—and near the front lines, no less.

Now that she was in Richmond, the local press ridiculed her for playing at being a man in a man's war. But deep down everybody probably feared her—because she was an affront to the very nature of American manhood. What nobody in town could have guessed was that Dr. Walker was ahead of her time—and well on her way to greatness.

Ahead of her time, Dr. Mary Edwards Walker earned leers and jeers for wearing pants. *Library of Congress.*

Dr. Mary Edwards Walker's unconventional path began in 1855, when the New York–born abolitionist became one of the first women to graduate from medical school. After a few months in Columbus, Ohio, she established a practice in Rome, New York, and married Albert Miller, also a physician, with whom she practiced but whose name she did not take. Both the practice and the marriage failed.

A women's rights activist, Dr. Walker had been an ardent supporter of women's dress reform under the leadership of Amelia Bloomer—the namesake of the trousers called "bloomers." Such feminists asserted that all those tight corsets and long heavy skirts were bad for women's health and limited the activities they could undertake.

Then the Civil War erupted. With the firm belief that "patriotism has no sex," Dr. Walker traveled to Washington, D.C. to join the Union army. She was denied a commission but stayed in Washington and worked as a volunteer nurse in a temporary hospital. Several months later, she was able to find work as a civilian contract field surgeon near the Union front lines in Virginia. Capable and tireless, she served at the front for almost two years.

In September 1863, Walker was appointed assistant civilian contract field surgeon for the Army of the Cumberland. She was apparently the only woman so engaged in the Civil War. Assigned to the Fifty-second Ohio Regiment, she quickly made herself a modified officer's uniform consisting of trousers, jacket and cavalry boots—and wore a pistol at each hip. Not surprisingly, Dr. Walker's arrival with the unit was met with disdain. The director of the medical staff considered the idea of a female surgeon a "medical monstrosity," and some of her patients were outraged that they weren't offered a male doctor. Dr. Walker continually crossed Confederate lines to treat civilians, possibly spying at the same time.

Her capture came on April 10, 1864, when she walked into a band of Confederate soldiers just south of the Georgia-Tennessee border. Several times, her captors offered her the opportunity of freedom. But there was one condition. She had to remove her manly dress and wear the hoop skirts of a "true woman." Sticking to her principles, she refused.

Once Dr. Walker landed in Castle Thunder Prison on Cary Street between Eighteenth and Nineteenth Streets, she was placed in the female ward. With diseases such as dysentery and smallpox prevalent in the prison, she instinctively went into activist mode. She treated some prisoners, as there was a chronic shortage of medical personnel. And after she insisted that fresh vegetables be added to the menu to ward off scurvy, the Confederates added cabbage to all the prisoners' rations.

Still, the *Richmond Examiner* took its insults to the extreme, referring to Dr. Walker as "Miss Doctress, Miscegenation, Philosophical Walker."[128]

In early July, after two months at the prison, Dr. Walker fell ill, plagued by an eye infection and "physical and emotional distress." She began petitioning for her freedom. By month's end, she appealed in person to Brigadier General William Montgomery Gardner, Richmond's new provost marshal. Gardner's leg had been shattered at First Manassas, leaving him crippled. To his surprise, he found Dr. Walker charming. He wrote of her as "the most personable and gentlemanly looking young woman I ever saw," adding that she gave evidence of "good birth and refinement as well as superior intellect." Nevertheless, he lectured her on the desirability of "feminine garb" and the futility of females serving in war. Dr. Walker gave it right back to him. She asserted that men had no business dictating to women on their garb and that women "consumed half their energies by carrying about a bundle of clothes."

In light of Dr. Walker's poor health, Gardner ordered her release on August 12, 1864. Also released were fourteen other Union doctors, in a prisoner exchange for Confederate surgeons. The *Richmond Dispatch* reported that "the notorious Miss Doctor Mary E. Walker" departed the city the morning of August 12 "in the steamer Schultz for Varina," where she would "take the flag-of-truce boat North."[129] Later, Dr. Walker proudly declared she was exchanged "man for man" with a tall Confederate major.

After Dr. Walker's recovery, she stumped for Abraham Lincoln's 1864 presidential campaign. In one speech, she said Lincoln's "great heart was constantly throbbing for the best interests of the most envied country in the World." After Lincoln's victory, she spent the remainder of the war providing care at a women's prison in Louisville and an orphan and refugee asylum in Tennessee.

Once the tremendous conflict was over, she was recommended for military recognition. Then, on November 11, 1865, President Andrew Johnson awarded Dr. Mary Edwards Walker the Congressional Medal of Honor for having "faithfully served as contract surgeon in the service of the United States, and [devoting] herself with much patriotic zeal to the sick and wounded soldiers, both in the field and hospitals, to the detriment of her own health." She was the first woman to receive this highest of military honors.

A year into peacetime, Dr. Walker happened to be at a hat shop in New York City, where her trousers attracted a mob on the sidewalk. After a defiant interchange with the police, she was arrested. Fighter that she was, she appealed the case in court.

"I wear this dress from high moral principle," she testified. "The fashionable dress of the day is not such as any physiologist can defend, nor any economist wear; it sweeps the filth from your sidewalks; it fastens the lungs as within a coffin, and encased within its iron bands no woman can venture out in a high wind, or attempt to climb a staircase, without immodest exposure of the limbs; it is an abomination, invented by the prostitutes of Paris, and as such unfit to be worn by a modest American woman..." Moments later, she added, "I claim in free America, on whose tented fields I have served four years in the cause of human freedom, the right unmolested to dress as I please."

The commissioner dismissed the case, saying, "Police have no more right to apprehend a woman in such a dress as hers than they have to arrest me." Then, turning to the officer, he said, "Let her go. She is smart enough to take care of herself. Never arrest her again." Dr. Walker departed from the courtroom under a storm of applause.[130]

In the late 1870s, Dr. Walker began wearing full male dress, including wing collar, bow tie and top hat. For the rest of her long life, she was devoted to the women's rights movement as a writer, lecturer and activist. Every step of the way, she proudly wore her war medal.

Chapter 12

MOONLIGHT COUNTERFEITERS

Facing the Wrath of the Confederate Court

Counterfeiters lurked behind nearly every lamppost in the Confederacy. But just one was executed. His name was John Richardson, alias Louis Napoleon.

Richmond newspapers chronicled the whole lurid tale. In late February 1862, "Italian adventurer" John Richardson bumped into an old acquaintance on Fourteenth Street in Richmond, named George Elam. After they downed a few pints at the corner saloon, Elam suggested they "go and make some money." Richardson agreed. In the dark of night, the pair skulked to the printing office of Hoyer and Ludwig at Twelfth and Main Streets. The firm had been retained by the Confederacy to print postage stamps and Treasury notes. Elam broke in and handed Richardson a pistol to "shoot anybody who might approach." On a table inside, they found eight sheets of ten-dollar notes.

"Here is money enough," Richardson whispered.

"Hush your mouth," Elam snapped. They put the $100 plate on the press and struck off a sweet $800 for each of them.

"Here is money enough," Richardson insisted, as Elam struck off a few more.

Minutes later, as the duo fled the scene, their plot was only half finished. Now they needed to forge signatures on the notes. Elam led Richardson to a shop near the Mayo Bridge, where they obtained a genuine note from which to copy the needed signatures.

The next day, forged notes began cropping up all over Richmond. Authorities quickly apprehended Richardson for passing a large amount of the "bogus money." Detectives learned that Elam "had been a party to the transaction" and tracked him down in Petersburg. In his trunk, just sent by rail from Richmond, the authorities found $690 in signed $10 bills and over $1,000 in unsigned notes. If that weren't damning enough, one of Elam's accomplices turned state's evidence on the scheme. Elam was thrown in a Petersburg jail, awaiting trial.

Meanwhile, Richardson was swiftly tried and convicted by the Confederate States Court. In early April, barely a month after the crime, he was sentenced to be "hung by the neck until dead." The editors of the *Dispatch* pronounced the sentence justified: "A whole nation is threatened with destruction by the doubt which the discovery of one forged note throws around its whole, its only currency." If confidence in the Treasury notes was undermined, the paper asserted, the entire Confederacy could "crumble away as the baseless fabric of a dream." There shouldn't be any sympathy for Richardson either, the paper argued, because he was "a doubly dyed scoundrel, skulking out" of the Confederate army by pleading Italian citizenship and, "worse still, striking at the very vitals of the Confederacy by forging that which is the only pay which she can give to her soldiers and creditors." To top it all off, the *Dispatch* took shots at his character, alleging, "Richardson is an Italian, of bad countenance, dissolute habits, and until recently was the proprietor of a little confectionary, as a blind for the illicit sale of poisonous liquors in the rear."[131]

President Davis granted Richardson a stay of execution—twice, in fact. But there were voices calling for Davis to make an example out of him, since other counterfeiters were "endeavoring to bring discredit on our currency by repeating Napoleon's offence [*sic*]."[132] On August 22, 1862, Richardson's luck finally ran out. He was to be hung that day in Shockoe Valley just east of the city's new almshouse—a site long used for public executions. At 10:45 that morning,

the jail doors opened, and the accused appeared, wearing a calm and self possessed air. He took off his hat and bowed to the crowd, who had assembled at the jail door, prior to seating himself on his coffin, which was in an ordinary furniture wagon. A detachment of Elliott's City Battalion, under Lieut. Johnson, then formed a hollow square around the vehicle, and the cortege wended its way up Valley street to the place of execution. A miscellaneous crowd, of perhaps a thousand persons, followed, including

*a number of painted and overdressed females of doubtful respectability.
Arriving at the ground, the condemned, with Deputy Marshal Myers and
Father Barratta, ascended to the platform and stood on the drop. Here over
half an hour was spent by the prisoner in conference with his spiritual
adviser; during which time he confessed the crime of which he had been
convicted. Five minutes before 12 o'clock, yielding himself to the officer,
he was made ready, and at 12 precisely the drop fell, leaving Richardson,
alias Napoleon, a dangling mass of inanimate clay, suspended between
the heavens and earth. He fell about four feet--a sufficient distance to have
broken his neck. But few convulsive twitchings were noticeable. After hanging
for 35 minutes he was pronounced dead, and the body being lowered, the
rope was carefully removed and the body put in a coffin.*[133]

Elam, on the other hand, didn't get a speedy trial. In March 1863, after
nearly a year of trial delays, he escaped from the Richmond City jail—right
under the nose of Company B, City Battalion.

Days later, on March 30, a member of the battalion spotted Elam entering
a restaurant on the south side of the Turning Basin. After gathering several
of his battalion comrades, the officers approached Elam and demanded
his surrender. Armed with a pistol, Elam fled from the restaurant, with the
officers in hot pursuit. Elam fired at them over his shoulder but missed. The
chase continued east along the Basin, between the two Gallego Flour Mills,
and to the Shockoe Warehouse. Elam frantically climbed through a window
and made his way to the attic, where he hid "in an old box that had formerly
been used to bring a horse from Petersburg." It only took a few minutes for
the officers to find him and draw their muskets. Elam surrendered, since
he'd dropped his pistol during the chase. He was thrown back in the city jail,
where they made sure he couldn't escape again.[134]

While awaiting trial, Elam was charged with assaulting two other "jail
birds."[135] For that crime, he was sentenced to a year in jail.

Elam was released in November 1864. His counterfeiting trial began in
February 1865, less than two months before the fall of Richmond.[136] With
his case having dragged on for so long, the *Dispatch* editors quipped they were
as nauseated with his name as with the phrase, "Foreign Intervention."[137]

It's unclear whether Elam was ever convicted or not, since his trail goes
cold in the papers. But it's likely that, before his case could be resolved, the
clock ran out on the Confederacy.

Chapter 13

THE BROOK CHURCH FIGHT

Forgotten Battle Claims Colonel James Byron Gordon

Renowned in Virginia are the Seven Days' Battles, the Battle of Seven Pines, and the two battles at Bull Run. Yet practically no one has heard of the Brook Church Fight just north of Richmond. Even people living in the neighborhood today are unaware that it took place, much less that the church itself even existed. When we forget these lesser battles, we're forgetting thousands of brave souls who died for their beliefs. A life is a life, whether it made headlines or not.

The modest and quaint Brook Church was built in 1787, amidst sweeping plantations and pristine countryside. Taking its name from Upham Brook, which snaked its course about a third of a mile to the west, it was erected by members of the neighboring community as a schoolhouse and "free church." (Unlike many churches of the time, its congregants didn't have to pay rent for their posteriors to occupy a pew.)

The structure went by several other names, including the Brook School House.[138] It stood southwest of today's intersection of Brook Road and Azalea Avenue—the current site of a gas station. There are no known photographs of Brook Church, but it apparently looked more like a schoolhouse than a church. In 1855, it was described as "a very neat, commodious building" by one of the ministers co-opting the space, J. Ambler Weed. He reported "an attentive and growing congregation, who unite with remarkable spirit in the services, although to many of them a novelty."[139] Most of the farmhouses in his little parish were scattered along Brook Turnpike—today's Brook Road.

Diligent and lovable, Reverend Weed probably doubled as the schoolteacher there. But in 1858, Protestants condemned him for committing the ultimate sin—"defecting" to the Catholic church.

That same year, wealthy John Stewart of the nearby Brook Hill Plantation decided to have a two-hundred-seat Episcopal church built on his land. It pained him to see his poor, rural neighbors "heathenized" and churchless, and he felt a duty to make good use of his wealth. Another motive, as his descendants tell it, was that the closest Episcopal Church was in the city—at least an hour and a half away by carriage—and he was tired of making the long trip every Sunday. To lead the fledgling Emmanuel Church, Stewart tapped longtime friend Richard Hooker Wilmer, a man "of great eloquence in the pulpit." Wilmer also happened to have another gift: he was a crack at billiards.

Firmly rooted in Virginia, Reverend Wilmer was a product of time and place. An ardent Southern sympathizer, he believed that slavery was "beneficial to the whites because it made them accustomed from childhood to responsibility and to the exercise of powers of command," and "beneficial

Richard Hooker Wilmer, preacher and slaveholder.
Richard Hooker Wilmer, Second Bishop of Alabama.

to the blacks whom it had lifted up from the savage state." Wilmer's wife had inherited a few slaves, and he bought others to keep them from falling into the hands of ruthless traders.

While construction on Emmanuel Church began in 1859, Reverend Wilmer held services about a quarter mile south at Brook Church, nicknamed "The Brook." He also knocked on doors in the neighborhood as a missionary. Stewart funded the spiritual groundwork as well as the new church building. Shortly after the foundation was laid, Wilmer proudly wrote Stewart of his growing flock: "We had a fine congregation at the Brook…many seatless, and fringing the outside of the windows."

Completed in 1860, the charming, Gothic Revival–style Emmanuel Church was nestled in a beautiful grove of pine trees along the Brook turnpike, "which unrolled itself like a long brown ribbon upon a robe of emerald."[140] As idyllic as this scene was, however, Virginia's political atmosphere was in turmoil and verging on all-out war.

Shortly after the fateful bombardment of Fort Sumter in mid-April 1861, Robert E. Lee arrived in Richmond. He accepted Governor Letcher's request to serve as major general in command of all Virginia's forces. Soon afterward, Reverend Wilmer asked him privately whether he thought the war would perpetuate slavery. "The future is in the hands of Providence," Lee said. "If the slaves of the South were mine, I would surrender them all without a struggle to avert the war."[141]

As Reverend Wilmer added a prayer for the president of the Confederacy to his liturgy, John Stewart's land saw another construction project— earthen fortifications. Built by slaves and free blacks along Brook Turnpike, just north of Brook Hill and Emmanuel Church, these earthworks were a critical part of the city's Outer Defenses. Their remnants still stand near Martin's Grocery Store, surrounded by a sea of asphalt.

In the latter part of the conflict, Union troops occasionally breached the defenses and unleashed hell along Brook Turnpike. The incursion on May 12, 1864, would go down in history as the "Brook Church Fight."

The day before, Confederate General J.E.B. Stuart was wounded during Sheridan's Raid near the Yellow Tavern, which stood about three miles north of Brook Church. He was rushed to Richmond for care. That evening, under cover of darkness and a heavy thunderstorm, Sheridan and his troops advanced southward on Brook Turnpike to wreak havoc in Richmond. They easily cleared the Outer Defenses, which were unmanned. But nipping at their heels for days was Confederate Colonel James B. Gordon, commander of all North Carolina cavalrymen. He had helped bring unparalleled success to Stuart's famed Confederate cavalry and was "largely responsible for Stuart's last battlefield victory."[142] Now, he needed to fill Stuart's shoes.

In the early morning hours of May 12, attempting to escape from Gordon's cavalry, Sheridan's troops turned east at Brook Church onto Military Road (today's Azalea Avenue) and set out for Meadow Bridge on the upper Chickahominy. With Gordon and his cavalry in hot pursuit, Sheridan placed one of his divisions in his rear along Military Road.

General James Byron Gordon. He was mortally wounded during the Brook Church Fight, which many historians have lumped with the Battle of Meadow Bridge. *Library of Virginia.*

Gunfire began shortly after daylight. Sheridan's men tried to keep the Confederates at bay with artillery and canister shot. Undaunted, Gordon dismounted a contingent of his cavalry and ordered them into line of battle. Then he dispatched one of his lieutenants to Richmond for artillery support. In the meantime, Gordon rode up and down his lines. When his men began receiving heavy return fire, an officer urged Gordon to dismount. "No," he bellowed, "we must set the men an example of gallantry to-day."

Fortunately, just minutes later, Confederate artillery reinforcements arrived from the city. They took position on the side of the Military Road atop some entrenchments and fired. Sheridan's guns returned the favor with a deadly barrage of canister shot, and mangled men fell left and right. Gordon's fighters didn't know it yet, but elements of three Virginia regiments and three companies from the City Batallion would soon arrive for support.

Mid-morning, with the Confederates in disarray and Gordon desperate to hold his position, he charged forward in a gallop—right into the fire. A ball struck his left arm, and he fell. Several men rushed to his side. Cheeringly, Gordon said he wasn't badly hurt and exhorted them to hold their ground.

Gordon was rushed by ambulance to the Officers' Hospital in Richmond near Tenth and Marshall Streets. Shortly after twelve noon, as rain fell, he was carried inside and operated on at once. The surgeons finished their work about the time the Confederates fell back at Brook Church, which was close to 4:00 that afternoon.

The next day, as a throng of Richmonders tearfully attended J.E.B. Stuart's funeral, Gordon seemed on the mend. But an infection set in. On May 18, six days after receiving his battle wound, General James B. Gordon was dead.

Now, the Confederates had one more brave leader to place at their altar. They named Gordon their own Joachim Murat—Napoleon's finest cavalry commander. "Enclosed in a box," Gordon's remains were escorted to the Danville rail depot by the Public Guard and band, then transported to his home state of North Carolina.[143] He was buried with full military honors. Perhaps North Carolina's best cavalryman ever, he was largely forgotten.

The Brook Church Fight left high casualties on the Confederate side. One of them was nineteen-year-old infantryman William G. Shough of Richmond, who'd joined Company D just two months earlier. Some of the wounded were carried to Brook Church and other places on the turnpike, with ambulances making runs to the city all day.[144]

Remarkably, two area citizens had joined the fight—an old man and his young son. The man brought his boy into line, and they fought like "veteran soldiers." The next day, a member of Gordon's brigade tossed them a bouquet, saying, "Would that their noble spirit could pervade the bosom of every man when his home is thus seriously endangered, and may their noble conduct be imitated by all should Richmond be again seriously menaced."[145]

Brook Church also served as a backdrop for other war dramas. It was used once as a hospital for "Yankee wounded," and on several occasions Confederate troops were quartered there.

But about two months after the Brook Church Fight, the historic structure went up in flames. "On last Sunday week, at night, some sacrilegious incendiary applied the torch to the Brook Church," the *Dispatch* reported on August 3, "and before the neighbors could assemble on the ground it was entirely destroyed." But Richmond historian Dr. H. Douglas Pitts stated it was accidentally burned by Confederate troops.[146]

While all traces of the Brook Church are long gone, Emmanuel Church still thrives. You can find it at the end of a long, winding road named after a divine billiards player.

Chapter 14

FOREIGN ASSISTANCE

French Novel Eases Confederate Miseries

S outherners ached. Food and clothing were hard to come by.
But even more painful to General George Pickett's wife, Sallie, was the shortage of good books. No longer was there a steady infusion of literature by top writers in the North and Europe because shipping was cut off. Many literature lovers in the Confederacy regarded "last week's newspaper as a gracious benefaction," Sallie said, and "a summer novel as an Olympian gift."

One day, Sallie finally got her hands on a sensational new work. She was elated. One of her friends in the U.S. Army had sent her, across the lines, a beautiful copy of the historical novel *Les Miserables*. It was written by the "high priest of romanticism," Victor Hugo. The title, which translates to "The Miserable Ones," had been published in France in 1862. It was a runaway hit in Europe.

The next year, thousands of Confederates happily shared in Sallie's good fortune. A Richmond publisher on Main Street, West & Johnston, had *Les Miserables* translated into English and printed it a few blocks down the street. West & Johnston was the most important press of the Confederacy,[147] and *Les Miserables* would become the most popular foreign novel in the fledgling nation. But this Confederate version was censored. It carefully omitted the passages reflecting Hugo's abolitionism. Also missing were several "rather rambling disquisitions on political and other matters of a purely local character...exclusively intended for the French readers of the book."

With wartime shortages of paper and ink, the book was a down-and-dirty production, dressed in a "Confederate garb of inferior ink, bad type, and worse paper."[148] The paper was thin, rough and flecked with trash—and was even used for the cover. Broken out into five volumes and printed over a two-year period, each pamphlet was offered at two dollars apiece.

In February 1863, West & Johnston glorified its new release in a *Richmond Dispatch* advertisement. "This novel has cost its gifted author twenty five years of his ripe genius," it raved, "and it is deemed the most finished and perfect Life Novel of modern times." Planning a wide circulation, the paper added, "It will be offered for sale by all Booksellers in the Confederate States."[149]

According to legend, the Confederacy issued the pamphlets to officers. Soldiers adored the volumes, sometimes reading them aloud to their comrades around the campfire. According to John Esten Cooke—the Richmond litterateur who served as J.E.B. Stuart's aide—*Les Miserables* even found its way to men in the trenches: "Everywhere, you might see the gaunt figures in their tattered jackets bending over the dingy pamphlets—'Fantine,' or 'Cosette,' or 'Marius,' or 'St. Denis,' and the woes of 'Jean Valjean,' the old galley-slave, found an echo in the hearts of these brave soldiers, immersed in the trenches and fettered by duty to their muskets or their cannon."

Cooke described how, during the grim Petersburg campaign of 1864, *Les Miserables* "whiled away the dreary hours of the old soldiers of Lee."[150] The story spoke to them. It was about another real-life rebellion—the Parisian June rebellion of 1832.

Many of Lee's soldiers didn't know how to pronounce the French title, and called it, "Lee's Miserables." Jokingly, they began calling *themselves* "Lee's Miserables," which spoke volumes about the horrible conditions during the war's final year. It helped them laugh at their miseries.

The confusion didn't end there. The *Richmond Whig* reported that an old lady sauntered into West & Johnston's bookstore and said, "I want a copy of that book about General Lee's poor miserable soldiers faintin'. The clerk had no clue what she was talking about. He sent for one of the proprietors, and had the lady repeat her request. The proprietor scratched his head for a moment, then exclaimed, "Oh! ah! yes! I know what it is now you mean. *Les Miserables*. Fantine by Victor Hugo."

"No, I don't," replied the old lady. "I know nothing and care nothing about Lays Meeserarbuls. I want Lee's Miserables faintin'." Turns out, she mistook the title for an official report about Lee's soldiers fainting in the field.[151] Irked and frustrated, she left the store in a huff.

Chapter 15

RICHMOND'S QUEEN OF HOSPITALITY

The Making of the City's Virtual Salon

A few days after soldier boy Robert reported to Richmond for duty, he got very ill. The poor, meager rations didn't help. When his marching orders came, some of his comrades urged him to stay behind in camp. But Robert rallied, dutifully heading out with the others on foot toward the rail depot. Before long, he nearly collapsed. An officer gave him permission to go the rest of the way by vehicle—if he could find one—assisted by a fellow soldier named Charley. So, as Robert held on to Charley's arm, the two men ambled in search of a hack driver.

Just then, Robert's eye was drawn to one of the most splendid residences he'd ever seen, at the southeast corner of Grace and Sixth Streets. Standing in the doorway was a lady about his mother's age, possessing an extraordinary radiance. "As soon as I caught the glance of her dark, lustrous and intelligent eye," Robert wrote home, "I read in an instant the history of a great and noble heart in her beautiful face." She glanced sympathetically back at him, in his weakened condition. In tones both soft and sweet, she asked Charley, "Why, young man, is not your friend sick? Surely, he is very sick, come, bring him into my house and let me do something for him, or send for a doctor."

Robert was deeply touched by her benevolence. He felt as if "an angel had come sailing down out of the skies and lit before us, and offered to fan my fevered brow with its golden wings." He and Charley warmly thanked the lady but insisted they had to "hurry forward."

For high-society Confederates, all roads led to Mrs. Stanard's elegant home at Sixth and Grace. *VCU Libraries.*

The lady knew better. "Hurry forward, indeed," she replied. "You are not able to go at all." With a warm smile and a graceful wave of her hand, she insisted the boys come inside. Mesmerized by her charms, they obeyed.

The beautiful, kind lady seated the soldiers in her elegant dining room and offered them some fine wine. It was "some of the most delicious wine I ever smacked a lip over," Robert wrote. Then came a hearty, delicious breakfast. Robert felt much better already. Finally the boys stood, expressed their gratitude and said they had to be on their way. The lady begged them to stay for a few days until Robert recovered, but they explained they had to make their train. After she packed them some scrumptious, home-cooked victuals for their journey, Robert felt like he'd been blessed with "the manna which was rained on the children of Israel in the wilderness."

Robert had to leave in such a rush that he regrettably didn't catch the kind lady's name. She was Mrs. Robert C. Stanard, renowned on both sides of the Atlantic for her special brand of warmth and hospitality.

Richmond legend Martha Pearce Stanard, at twenty-five. Painted by English miniaturist George L. Saunders. *The Filson Historical Society, Louisville, Kentucky.*

Born Martha Pearce in 1820 into a wealthy family in Louisville, Kentucky, she blossomed into a remarkable beauty. "Tall and stately in figure," she was educated at Madame Chegaray's School for Young Ladies in Manhattan.[152] Considered the most fashionable finishing school for girls in the country—"embracing the Latin, English and French languages"— it would shape her adult life. At fifteen, while traveling alone through Washington, D.C. "under the care of Henry Clay," she was introduced to handsome Richmond lawyer Robert C. Stanard on the steps of the Capitol. A year later they were married, and Martha entered Richmond society.

Robert inherited the mansion on Grace Street from his father, filled with exquisite furnishings from Italy and Paris. The frescoed ceilings were "worthy of a royal palace."[153] Robert and Martha's home "early became noted for hospitality as lavish as it was elegant."[154] Due in no small measure to Martha's refinement and "brilliant intellect," their guests were the cultured, wealthy elites and literary luminaries of the South. In 1853, they feted their friend, British novelist William Makepeace Thackeray, who was in Richmond to lecture on "English Humourists of the Eighteenth Century." The Stanards also rolled out the red carpet for countless jurists and politicians, as Mr. Stanard became prominent in the higher courts of the state and served a term in the Virginia Senate.

After he died in 1857, Martha—"a widow of ample means"—continued her reign.[155] One source said, "Around her in her elegant drawing-rooms she gathered a wonderful coterie—statesmen, belles and beaux of the day—all delighting in Mrs. Stanard's delightful wit and adroit repartee."[156] By the eve of war, her home reached even higher acclaim. In his book, *Belles, Beaux and Brains of the Sixties,* Thomas C. DeLeon said, "What came nearest to a salon in Richmond—and, as far as I know in all America—was held at Mrs. Robert C. Stanard's."[157]

By definition, her gatherings had all the elements of a French salon—except they weren't in France, of course. The guests were highly distinguished, socially and intellectually. The conversation was for amusement as well as to spread knowledge and refine their taste in literature and the arts. And most importantly, perhaps, there was an inspiring hostess at the center of it all. Since Mrs. Stanard was well traveled and had many well-known literary friends around the globe, she may very well have visited the salons of France herself.

Social life in Richmond didn't come to a halt under the stress of war. Mrs. Stanard made sure of that, despite the massive "invasion" of strangers to the city. Her drawing room became "a meeting point for the official life of the Confederacy, and her wartime breakfasts and luncheons were greatly appreciated social affairs."[158] DeLeon echoed these sentiments, saying, "At her frequent dinners, receptions and evenings, Mrs. Stanard collected most that was brilliant and brainiest in government, army, congress and the few families who followed either, apparently because they could afford to."

Beautiful, gracious and witty, Mrs. Stanard mastered the art of entertaining. She didn't simply fling open her doors to a long list of guests with distinguished pedigrees. She chose them "studiously for what was in them," as well as "their adaptability to each other."[159]

One who passed the test was Judah P. Benjamin, the third Confederate secretary of state. An "intellectual phenomenon," he brought "his charming stories, his dramatic recitation of scraps of verse, and clever comments on men, women, and books."[160]

Also gracing Mrs. Stanard's parlors was Wade Hampton, a superior Confederate Cavalry officer and wealthy South Carolina plantation owner. Possessing a "high intelligence and superb physique," he was a former South Carolina senator. In the early days of war, he organized and financed the infamous military unit Hampton's Legion. As the unit was marching off to war through Petersburg in early July 1861, the *Dispatch* reported that the "splendid body of men…are all young, and most of them occupy high social positions at home. The whole Legion comprises about eleven companies, and thirteen hundred men."[161]

General Wade Hampton, who'd inherited one of the largest collections of slaves in the South. *Library of Congress.*

Then there was Confederate senator Thomas Jenkins Semmes. As chairman of the joint committee on the flag and seal of the Confederate States, he wrote its motto, *Deo Vindice*. In Latin, it translates to "God is our vindicator." Perhaps he told Mrs. Stanard's guests his rationale in choosing those words: "In the spirit of the lapidary style of composition, [they] were elliptical and left much to the play of the imagination."[162]

Another prominent Confederate cabinet member in the crowd was John Archibald Campbell, a former judge of the U.S. Supreme Court. A child prodigy, he was Jefferson Davis's choice for assistant secretary of war in 1862. Three times he tried to negotiate peace—once right before the "collision," once during the Confederacy's final months and again immediately after the evacuation of Richmond.

Mingling with this elite group was one of Mrs. Stanard's close friends, Richmond litterateur and refined gentleman John R. Thompson. He served as assistant secretary of the commonwealth in the Confederate cabinet and was a leading war poet. Full of entertaining anecdotes, he was known to put "everybody in a good humor with his sparkling witticisms and the point and finish of his discourse."[163] He sought Mrs. Stanard's "keen yet sympathetic criticism" on his works.[164] Here's an excerpt from his poignant war poem, "Music In Camp":

> *As fades the iris after rain*
> *In April's tearful weather,*
> *The vision vanished as the strain*
> *And daylight died together.*
>
> *But Memory, waked by Music's art,*
> *Exprest in simplest numbers,*
> *Subdued the sternest Yankee's heart,*
> *Made light the Rebel's slumbers.*

Another man lending "the witchery of his presence" at Mrs. Stanard's was Lucius Quintus Cincinnatus Lamar. After writing the official Mississippi Ordinance of Secession, he funded the Nineteenth Mississippi Volunteer Infantry, for which he bravely served as lieutenant colonel. In 1862, Jefferson Davis appointed him Confederate Minister to Russia and special envoy to England and France. His charm, manners and oratory made him a hit in London.[165]

Even President Jefferson Davis and Vice President Alexander H. Stephens were numbered among Mrs. Stanard's guests.

Fittingly, Mrs. Stanard's salon included the man with a poetic name, Lucius Quintus Cincinnatus Lamar. *Library of Congress.*

It's no wonder that so many mature men thronged to Mrs. Stanard's drawing room. She was in her early forties and "beautiful and agreeable still."[166]

Which brings us to one of her more frequent guests, Pierre Soulé, the Franco-American revolutionary and former U.S. Minister to Spain. He was best known for his role in writing the Ostend Manifesto in 1854, which proposed the purchase of Cuba from Spain. As a Confederate, he was briefly imprisoned at Fort Lafayette in New York and then fled to Nassau and Havana. In 1863, he sought a military appointment from the Confederate government. But there was bad blood between President Davis and Soulé, so he ended up with an honorary brigadier-generalship. Still, the "dark, suave, and courtier-like" Soulé, with his pronounced French accent, wooed Mrs. Stanard. There was talk of marriage, and Mrs. Stanard had "wedding finery" shipped by flag of truce.[167] In the end, however, she decided to call it off. She told her closest friends that when Soulé was with her, "he was so eloquent that she could not say no to him." But when he was away, she "realized what a mistake she would make in marrying a man upwards of sixty, who had no future before him."[168]

Not all of Mrs. Stanard's guests were male elders. She also opened her home to "the best of her own sex" and "the most polished and promising

"Old man eloquent," Pierre Soulé, who nearly talked Mrs. Stanard into marriage. *Library of Congress.*

of the youth of war."[169] They included the dashing and handsome Kyd Douglas, a staff officer for Stonewall Jackson who would author *I Rode With Stonewall*; the handsome and "intrepid" Major John B. Castleman, a rising star put in charge of an expedition to liberate all the Confederate prisoners in Illinois and Indiana; and Lord "Lordy" King, a Yale graduate and gallant officer known for daring reconnaissance missions. Mrs. Stanard's lady guests included Mary Chesnut, whose husband was a military aide to President Davis, and perhaps Mrs. George W. Randolph, whose husband was secretary of war.

As Mrs. Stanard's dignified guests engaged in lofty discussion about literature and art, luxuriating in her mansion's rich and classical appointments, they escaped the grimness of war. Of course, there must have been plenty of war talk, too.

It's been said that Mrs. Stanard's true "idol" was her only son, the "young, bright, gentlemanlike, and handsome," Captain Hugh M. Stanard.[170] Commended for his "devoted and gallant services" by General John B. Magruder, he bravely led troops at First Manassas.

In 1862, Mrs. Stanard sold her home at Sixth and Grace and moved to Eighth Street, a block west of the Capitol. While she happily took her salon with her, the move would prove a fateful decision. On April 3, 1865, as Richmond's evacuation fire inched toward her home and the city was gripped by panic, she was seen on the sidewalk, sitting on a trunk of hastily packed possessions. Viewing the horrific nightmare through her lorgnette, she refused assistance. Mrs. Stanard's home was said to be the last one burned that day.[171] Her former home at Sixth and Grace, just two blocks west, was unscathed.

After the Confederate defeat, Mrs. Stanard escaped to Europe for a time. There she received "the most devoted attention" from British diplomat and litterateur Sir Henry Bulwer and his wife. Mrs. Stanard had entertained the couple at her home, according to the 1867 book *The Queens of American Society.*

If Mrs. Stanard wanted to put the Union victory completely behind her, she could have heeded one of Bulwer's famous quotes: "Anger ventilated often hurries towards forgiveness; anger concealed often hardens into revenge."

Chapter 16

THE DREADED WHIPPING POST

Punishment Ordered in Mayor Mayo's Court

There's simply no denying it. Richmond slaves and free blacks were well acquainted with the rawhide lash.

Rooted in the mother country, the practice of whipping was enshrined in Virginia law. In 1661, the Virginia legislature mandated that all Virginia counties "sett up a pillory, a pair of stocks, and a whipping post, neere the courthouse." Shortly after the first Henrico County Courthouse was built in 1752 near today's intersection of Main and Twenty-second Streets, Richmond erected its whipping post, stocks and pillory at the public marketplace nearby. On that site today, believe it or not, is our folksy farmers' market. There at the public whipping post, criminals were whipped in front of onlookers and neighbors, with humiliation considered part of the punishment. The infamous Richmond Black Code mandated whippings for even minor offenses.

Before and during the Civil War, the daily *Richmond Dispatch* provided a list of petty criminals, their alleged offenses and the corresponding number of lashes ordered as punishment—as if it were infotainment. Since a police court hadn't yet been established, cases went straight to the court of popular Richmond mayor Joseph Mayo at city hall. As appalling as it sounds, he promised to "whip every nigger in the city."[172] On November 1, 1860, the paper reported that a slave named John "was arraigned before the Mayor yesterday, on a charge of stealing a piece of calico from his master, Joseph Rosenbaum." Since John admitted his guilt, "little time was occupied in disposing of his case, and he was sentenced to thirty lashes." On November

27, the paper reported, "Two negroes, named Harrison and George, slaves of C.P. Word, got into a fight on Sunday about a five cent piece, but were interrupted by the police, and yesterday received the reward of their valor at the whipping post." And on November 29, the paper said, "Sarah, slave of E.A.J. Clopton, was awarded 20 lashes…for using insulting and threatening language to Ann Wells and her sister."[173]

In March 1861—after Lincoln's inauguration but before Virginia seceded—the paper gave a particularly chilling report. "Samuel Gaines, free, arrested for getting drunk and lying in the street, thought 'Massa Lincoln would give him his rights,' whereupon the Mayor gave him 20 as a first instalment on Lincoln's behalf."[174]

Amid wartime emergency in the Confederate capitol, whippings under Mayor Mayo's rule became a regular, if not daily, occurrence. Here's merely a sampling, if you can stomach it. On August 29, 1861, the paper reported that "his Honor" had sentenced "John, slave of John A. Mayo" to fifteen lashes for walking the streets without a pass. The next week, a hack driver named John "was hauled up and ordered twenty lashes for breaking an engagement he had entered in, to carry a passenger to a prescribed place." In December 1862, "Billy, slave of Charles L. Stewart was brought up charged with stealing at various times from Jno. O'Neal, a quantity of bacon, lard and molasses" and was ordered twenty lashes. And in February 1863, "Minor, slave of James Brooks," was ordered five lashes "for being found smoking in the street."[175]

Right after Confederate president Jefferson Davis declared martial law in Richmond in March 1862, the *Dispatch* editor reminisced about the city's peaceful past. His words spoke volumes about race relations and the culture of the whipping post. "Our own city, before the beginning of the war, was the most quiet, and orderly city of its size in America, with the exception, perhaps, of Charleston," he began. "Its streets were as silent at night as any rural district in the country—not a sound was to be heard, save the deep roar of the river as it rushed over the falls…" There was no need for night watchmen back then, he said, except "now and then to participate in the arrest of some predatory African, who would be escorted at sunrise to the Mayor by the whole body of the guardians of the night, each looking majestically indignant at the violator of the law…After introducing the offender to the whipping post, there was a general dispersion of the city functionaries of high and low degree till the next morning." With the war now an ugly reality, the editor looked back with fondness to those "calm and somewhat monotonous days."[176]

Mayor Mayo wasn't the only man in the city sentencing blacks to the whipping post, as some of his rulings were appealed to the Hustings Court. But its decisions could be just as grim. "Woodson, Henry, and Albert, slaves, charged with breaking into the store of John O'Niel and stealing five kegs of lard, were tried," said the *Dispatch* on February 12, 1864, "whereupon the Court discharged Woodson and sentenced Henry and Albert each to receive nine and thirty lashes to be well laid on at the public whipping post." Whippings also occurred ad nauseum at the slave jails.

The whipping post, as depicted by John Mitchell Jr., the editor of the *Richmond Planet*. *www.lva.virginia.gov/exhibits/mitchell/cartoon.htm.*

During the war, the whipping post from what was called the "negro jail" in Portsmouth, Virginia, was taken to upstate New York as a war trophy by Private Charles C. Miller of Company I of the 148th New York Volunteers. He was a committed abolitionist. Eventually, it was donated to the Virginia Historical Society, which put it on display.[177]

It's unknown what became of Richmond's dreaded whipping post.

Chapter 17

FANFARE AT ROCKETTS WHARF

Arrival of Confederate Prisoners of War

It was a hellish day, at least for President Davis. On April 30, 1864, his beautiful, four-year-old son, Joseph, fell from a balcony at the Confederate White House and died. Wrought with anguish, the president kept repeating, "Not mine, oh, Lord, but thine."

Meanwhile, unaware of this tragedy, hundreds of Richmonders gathered for a joyful celebration down at Rocketts Wharf. About 350 sick and wounded Confederate prisoners were due to arrive by steamboat from City Point (now Hopewell). It was all part of a prisoner of war exchange with the Union army. The crowd of citizens waiting at shore's edge that warm and breezy afternoon were, said the *Dispatch*, "anxious to extend a cordial welcome to the brave boys who have been so long suffering the hardships of prison life in different parts of Yankeedom."[178] Even the Armory Band had come down to greet the men with fitting ceremonies.

Most of the incoming prisoners were complete strangers to the crowd. But that was beside the point. These Confederates had not only endured wretched conditions at Union prisons but were also "heroes of many a fight."

In recent weeks, the Union exchange officials had carefully screened the men, making sure they wouldn't go right back into the fight. Not making the cut was General Isaac R. Trimble—even though he'd lost his left leg at Gettysburg. His exchange got Abraham Lincoln's personal stamp of approval, but then something mysteriously went awry. In a possible flight of fancy, the *Dispatch* reported:

Rocketts Wharf, where hundreds of prisoners of exchange of both sides came and went by side-wheel steamer. *Library of Congress.*

…on reaching [Trimble's] *case the officer having the matter in charge telegraphed President Lincoln what should be done about it. Lincoln's reply was to ascertain whether he would be likely to enter the Confederate service if sent home. Upon interrogating the General as to his ability to do so, the old patriot, not understanding the trick, with his usual candor, promptly answered, "Oh, yes! I think I am in a condition to enter the service," whereupon he was ordered to stand aside.*[179]

Finally, the ones cleared for exchange—about fifty of them officers—traveled on a flag-of-truce boat from Fort Monroe to a way station at City Point. Then, on the morning of April 30, two Confederate side-wheel steamers—the *Schultz* and the *William Allison*—departed Rocketts Wharf in Richmond to pick up the men. Formerly James River cruisers, the "staunch little steamers" often chugged in tandem to transport exchanged prisoners of both sides.

One of the prisoners waiting at City Point was Colonel Archibald C. Godwin. Formerly provost marshal of Richmond and the namesake of the capital's

Among the returning prisoners of war was the six-foot-six, refined gentleman, Colonel Archibald C. Godwin. He had the dubious honor of having a prison named after him in the Confederate Capital. *Library of Congress.*

Castle Godwin prison, he was captured at Rappahannock Bridge. Another officer was Lieutenant Colonel John J. Jolly of the Forty-third Alabama Regiment, who was severely wounded at Chickamauga. Other officers hailed from states throughout the South.

Once the pair of steamers arrived in City Point, the paroled prisoners filed aboard under close Union guard.

Among the enlisted was infantryman John C. English of the Twenty-second Georgia Regiment, who had been captured at Gettysburg. He was considered too ill to make the trip. But he insisted, wanting "to die among his friends and sympathizers." Tragically, he didn't get his wish. He died aboard the *Allison* as it steamed toward the Confederate capital.

The crowd at Rocketts Wharf had no idea what time to expect the men. Hours passed, and the late day sun turned to darkness. Finally, around 8:30 p.m., the stillness was broken by the clang of the wharf bell, signaling that the steamers had appeared in the final bend of the river.

As the steamboats drifted up to the wharf, the crowd erupted with cheers, and the prisoners joined the happy chorus. The Armory Band heightened the glee, with its peppy, martial strains. Everyone was overjoyed. The men had finally reached freedom.

As the hundreds of men came ashore, some had large bandages and others hobbled on crutches. After a flurry of hugs, handshakes and congratulatory speeches, the men needed to check in to Confederate hospitals. So, led by the Armory Band and its merry music—and swelling with fresh optimism—they paraded off into the night.

Chapter 18

BECKMAN'S SALOON DOWN ON MAIN

A Snapshot of the City's Underbelly

W here there's smoke, there's fire. And where there's beer, there's trouble—especially if it's tapped in a seedy section of a war capital.

Beckman's saloon and restaurant stood on Main Street between Seventeenth and Eighteenth Streets, near the First Market House. The area crawled with pickpockets, alcoholic whores and cutthroats. Henry Beckman, the keeper of the saloon, had his share of barroom brawls, shady dealings and run-ins with the law.

"Lager beer—however popular as a beverage—often gets its imbibers into trouble," began the *Richmond Dispatch*, describing a summer 1863 incident at Beckman's establishment. A man named Henry Lepkar drank "a few mugs of the malt liquor," exchanged heated words with Beckman, "threw half a mug of beer into his face, and then smashed the mug over his head."[180]

The following January, police were tipped off to a suspicious pile of goods in Beckman's back room. The tin boxes, valued at $350 each, were believed to belong to the Confederate government. Mr. A. Berile, a "young man of rather genteel appearance," was suspected of trying to sell the tin. Police took him into custody and "lodged him in the lock-up for examination."[181]

Law enforcement was very familiar with the path to Beckman's door. There are stories of "drunkenness and disorderly conduct" and patrons trying to sell "hot" goods. Once, a man staggered in drunk and threatened to kill another patron. Some patrons took their disputes outside, resulting in robberies and shootings. One patron even shot at a police officer right in the doorway but missed.[182]

Then, in the summer of 1864, the saloon proprietor himself was thrown in the hoosegow. It wasn't just any hoosegow either—it was the dreaded Castle Thunder prison. "Henry Beckman, of lager beer saloon notoriety, was lodged in the Castle Tuesday, upon the charge of 'shirking' military duty," began the *Examiner*. It seemed too convenient that he claimed to have "a game leg." Beckman was hardly the only man pulling such stunts. "Several other parties, aspirants to the same honours, were lodged in the Castle with him to keep him company," the paper quipped.[183]

Beckman's harrowing experience at the Castle should have scared him straight. But it wasn't his nature. In March 1865, he was charged with selling liquor without a license and fined sixty dollars.

About two weeks later, Richmond was captured by the Federals. Beckman's saloon narrowly escaped the Evacuation Fire. Most the other saloons in the city were wiped out—as was much of the food supply—so Beckman's may have been one of the very few places to find some desperately needed sustenance. Perhaps Henry Beckman ended up a war hero after all.

Chapter 19

GEORGE ARENTS AND THE LINCOLN CONSPIRACY

Rumors Fly About Local Merchant

L ike his uncle, Lewis Ginter, George Arents grew up in New York before putting down deep roots in antebellum Richmond. But while both men were destined to become avid Confederates, Arents was implicated in a plot to kidnap President Lincoln.

Shortly before the war, as the nation was being torn apart by the heated debate over slavery, Ginter was running his wholesale fancy goods store at the southeast corner of Thirteenth and Main Streets. Around 1859, he brought in Arents, his energetic twenty-one-year-old nephew, as partner. The firm changed its name to Ginter, Alvey & Arents and became the "largest dry-goods and notions-house south of Philadelphia." With Richmond's economy booming, the store made Arents a member of Richmond's wealthy elite—that is, if he wasn't already.

When Lincoln was elected president in 1860, many Southerners in Arents's social class were outraged. The *Richmond Whig* said Lincoln's election "is undoubtedly the greatest evil that has ever befallen this country. But the mischief is done, and the only relief for the American people is to shorten sail...send down the top masts, and prepare for a hurricane."

In January 1861, the *Richmond Dispatch* lamented the economic repercussions in the South: "The merchants of Richmond alone have lost many thousands—we may safely say hundreds of thousands—of dollars by the money panic which the election of Lincoln has produced."[184] Hit especially hard were merchants dealing in luxury items, like Ginter, Alvey & Arents—angering them even further.

That April, Richmond was turned upside-down by the bombardment of Fort Sumter. President Lincoln ordered thousands of troops to crush the rebellion in the South. "Lincoln declares war on the South and his Secretary demands from Virginia a quota of cutthroats to desolate Southern firesides," said the *Richmond Examiner.*

Lincoln also instituted the blockade of Southern ports and targeted Southern slavery. White Richmonders fumed, declaring the president a "tyrant" and "despot." Just days later, Arents enlisted in the Howitzers Battalion of Light Artillery, serving under George Wythe Randolph, grandson of Thomas Jefferson.

For now, Ginter, Alvey & Arents stayed afloat. In the early months of the war, while Arents was serving in the Howitzers, the firm supplied Confederates with wool shawls, hats, blankets and materials for fashioning uniforms. It even supplied sheaths for swords, called scabbards.[185] The war was definitely good for business, at least in the beginning.

But anger toward President Lincoln continued to snowball. After the first major battle of the war at Manassas in July 1861, the *Richmond Enquirer* blamed Lincoln for all the deaths on both sides. "Of these men Abraham Lincoln is the murderer," the paper declared. "We charge their blood upon him…May the Heavens, which have rebuked his madness thus far, still battle his demon designs."[186]

Like many Southern businessmen, George Arents suffered greatly under Lincoln's war policies. Richmond Times, *April 2, 1901.*

That October, after six months on the battlefield, Arents hired a substitute and returned to Richmond to run the fancy goods store. After he enrolled in the local defense troops, a judge exempted him from conscription since he was a "mail contractor" when the Conscription Act was passed.[187]

In 1862, Ginter, Alvey & Arents owned a male slave, valued at $800.[188] Most likely he did the manual labor, such as lading and warehousing the imported cargo and keeping the store neat and clean. Because Arents owned "property" like this, he had some skin in the game.

By May 1862, the tide had turned against the Confederates, and it was clear the fighting would go on for years. Richmond's economy faltered again, with the added bite of wild inflation. Stores like Ginter, Alvey & Arents were doomed. Lewis Ginter entered the Confederate army as a commissary and soon sold his interest in the fancy goods store.

Upper-class Richmonders blew a gasket that September, when Lincoln issued his first Emancipation Proclamation. The *Examiner* decried it as "the call for the insurrection of four millions of slaves, and the inauguration of a reign of hell upon earth!"[189]

By early 1863, Arents formed a partnership with George J. Sumner, running an auction house in the former Ginter, Alvey & Arents building. The firm of Sumner & Arents sold blockade goods of every description, from organdy muslins and fancy soaps to pipes and pen holders.[190]

Meanwhile, the Confederates were at wit's end, looking for any way to gain the upper hand in the struggle. Then, in the summer of 1863, a devilish plot was reportedly hatched. It was all spelled out in the *New-York Tribune* by a former clerk at the War Department in Richmond, who escaped to his native North. He reported that "a club or society of wealthy citizens of Richmond" had been collecting funds to kidnap President Lincoln and hold him hostage in Richmond. "Sumner & Arents, auctioneers, subscribed $5,000," he claimed, and the local banking firm of R.H. Maury & Co. subscribed $10,000. The correspondent added that "circulars were sent to trustworthy citizens in every other city and town in the Confederacy, inviting co-operation in the grand undertaking, and an immense sum of money was subscribed." When all was ready, they planned to obtain a furlough for the guerrilla cavalry leader John S. Mosby and make him leader of the mission. "Whether these schemes have been abandoned, or whether the kidnappers are only awaiting a favorable opportunity to execute them, remains to be seen," warned the correspondent, "but certain it is that too much caution cannot be observed by the President, or the military commanders stationed at the capital."[191]

The Democratic press fired back, calling the claims patently false. But the *Tribune* correspondent said he had proof. He produced a letter from a Confederate officer in North Carolina, Calhoun Cullum, that had been sent to a clerk in the war office in Richmond. Dated September 30, 1863, Cullum referred to the "ruse de guerre" to capture Lincoln and said, "I would willingly sell my soul to the devil for the honor of playing a conspicuous part in the destruction of the *great hydra*." He signed off by pleading, "Don't neglect me."

Ultimately, in April 1865, President Lincoln did end up in Richmond. But it was entirely on his own accord. The city had just fallen, and the Union's commander-in-chief strode through the streets to survey the burned-out capitol. The newly freed slaves had a jubilee in the streets, while many devastated whites stayed in their homes with shutters drawn. Just days later, Lincoln was assassinated in Washington by John Wilkes Booth.

The next year, as it turned out, the *Tribune* correspondent was charged with perjury and sentenced to prison. Suddenly, his story about the Richmond plot was cast in doubt, even though it seemed too detailed to be made up. But there had certainly been kidnapping conspiracies much like the one he outlined.

As the door slammed shut on the correspondent's prison cell, both Lewis Ginter and George Arents were on course to regain their former wealth. They had become bankers and brokers in New York City. In the mid-1870s, Ginter became a pioneer in the cigarette industry, and in 1889, he helped form the American Tobacco Company. Arents became the company's longtime treasurer. Ginter died in 1897 with an estate valued at about $2 million.

In the new century, with the exploding popularity of the cigarette, Arents's wealth surpassed that of his deceased uncle. Combined with many other business ventures, including the Jefferson Hotel and real estate development in Richmond's Fan District and Ginter Park, the New Yorker died in 1918 with a net worth of $10 million. Naturally, the vast majority of his portfolio was in tobacco.[192]

To this day, no one knows if George Arents helped fund the kidnapping plot or not. It's interesting to note, however, that as the plot was reportedly being financed in the summer of 1863, George was grieving the loss of his twenty-three-year-old brother, Frederick, who had just been violently killed while serving the Confederacy. He was aboard CSS *Chattahoochee* in Florida when its boiler exploded.

Chapter 20

AVENGING THE "TRAITORESS"

Rush to Judgment for Mary Caroline Allan

Absolute devotion to the cause was sacrosanct in the Confederate capital. The slightest whiff of Union sentiment in the air could trigger a full-fledged witch hunt. Which brings us to the story of Mary Caroline Allan, charged with high treason. The evidence against her seemed compelling—and Richmonders demanded swift, severe punishment. The only thing that could save her was a miracle. And that's practically what she got.

The incredible story opens in July 1863 at the Richmond gambling establishment of William Burns. It doubled as a "depot" of underground mail headed North by blockade runner. Burns came across an envelope, addressed, "Miss H. Haines, New York. In haste." For some reason, he opened it. Inside he found another envelope, addressed to "Rev. Morgan Dix"—the son of Union General John Dix. Smelling a rat, Burns tore into that envelope and read the enclosed letter. He was horrified. It divulged the identities of Northerners who supported the Confederate cause; contained maps showing "commanding locations" on the James River where Federal guns should be placed; and targeted Richmond's beloved divine, Reverend Moses D. Hoge, who was in Europe securing thousands of Bibles for the Confederate troops. The letter asserted that Hoge's mission was just a pretext—that he was actually trying to stir up European support for the Confederate cause. It even supplied the date Reverend Hoge was due back in America and urged Union officials to capture him upon his return and confine him in a dark dungeon for the rest of the war. Dated June 8, 1863, the letter began, "*Caro Signore*," Italian for *Dear Sir:*

> *I humbly entreat you will hasten to inform your father of the contents of this letter. Oh! friend, in these days of terror, despotism, and despondency, one seeks in vain for sympathy in these regions of secession, where every heart seems filled with hatred, malice, and revenge; where one hears young women talk of turning over, on battle-fields, "horrid, nasty, grinning skulls of Yankees," with their dainty feet. Then, for the sake of your country, do what you can to arrest all instigators and abettors of this rebellion. Tell your father that about the 11th of this month the Rev. M.D. Hoge will attempt to run the blockade from St. Thomas to Charleston. He has been for sometime past in London, where his apparent business was to collect testaments and bibles, but where his real object was to write for English journals and exert his influence for the Southern cause. A greater rebel firebrand does not exist.*

After naming Hoge's friends and Southern sympathizers in the North, the author referred to General Stoneman's recent raid in Virginia. The author lamented that the general had failed to seize the "plantations of several of the most prominent rebels" in Goochland County, including that of Secretary of War Seddon. Lastly came a passionate appeal:

> *Oh, sir! the universal cry here is to raise the black flag. Oh! for the hour when the avenging angel shall appear, with torch in one hand and the avenging sword of justice in the other, and consecrate to death and destruction this land and these people, rewarding them with a fate they so richly deserve! When, when will that time arrive? The women and preachers are amongst the most earnest and determined rebels in the South. They do more to stimulate and keep alive the spirit of rebellion than any other members of society. Many a man wearing the Federal uniform is a traitor, and where the men are true their wives are false. It is this which has so often proved ruinous to the Union cause. Here, every mind, heart and arm are bent to the cause of the South. Money, property, crops, everything, is sacrificed for the main idea. Thus the South has been able to maintain its position thus far...Oh, friend, watch well, and, I beseech thee, allow no appearance of Southern sympathy in your presence. This letter would be my death warrant if discovered.*

The letter was signed with the alias *Santa Trinita*.

Burns rushed the treasonous letter to Judge Ould, the Confederate prison-exchange commissioner. He wanted to find out who wrote it—and *fast*—so he asked Burns to track down the man who delivered it to him. Before long, Burns returned with the whole story. The letter had been passed off several times, but—according to his source—it originated from a lady named Mrs. Patterson Allan.[193] Otherwise known as Mary Caroline Allan, her husband was the wealthy Goochland County plantation owner Patterson Allan, who happened to be the son of Edgar Allan Poe's foster father.

There was even more to implicate Mrs. Allan's guilt. Burns had ripped into another letter, addressed to her sister in Cincinnati. It called General Stoneman the "white gloved" general and criticized his leniency toward the Confederates. To Burns, the handwriting on the two letters looked identical.

Swiftly, Judge Ould sent the letters to Confederate secretary of war James A. Seddon—who forwarded them to Richmond's provost marshal, General John H. Winder. He swept into action. Aware that Mrs. Allan was visiting with the Hoge family, he dispatched his team of detectives to their home at the northeast corner of Fifth and Main Streets. But it was horrible timing. When they arrived, they found three-year-old Lacy Hoge lying dead inside, awaiting burial. He had died from a painful infection, the result of a stubbed toe while playing. Out of consideration for the family, Winder had the detectives postpone the arrest. But Mrs. Allan was "instructed to consider herself within the meshes of military law," and the detectives were ordered to keep "watch and ward over the house."[194]

On July 18, after little Lacy's funeral, General Winder headed straight to the home to arrest Mrs. Allan himself. He knocked on the door, and a servant answered. Mrs. Allan was sent for, and moments later she stepped into the parlor to meet him. The cold-eyed general lowered the boom, outlining his suspicions and flashing the letter in her face. But Mrs. Allan denied any knowledge of it. Calmly, Winder told her to think again and tell him the truth. Raising up her hands, Mrs. Allan bellowed, "I swear, I know nothing about it!"[195]

Aroused by the clamor, Mrs. Hoge entered the room. Mrs. Allan swept toward her, asking if she considered her capable of such a thing. When Mrs. Hoge assured her that she believed in her innocence, Mrs. Allan cried, "I would not have written such a letter about Mr. Hoge, whom I have always regarded as my best friend. I swear I never wrote that letter, nor do I know anything of its contents!"[196] Winder was unmoved.

Soon thereafter, Mrs. Allan claimed that the "Santa Trinita" letter had been given to her "servant man John" by a white man who requested that

Mrs. Allan forward it north for him. While Winder followed up on this lead, he kept guards around the Hoge home.

A few days later, Mrs. Hoge asked that some other arrangements be made, as it was "unpleasant to have a police force constantly watching the movements of her family." General Winder was known to toss suspects right into Castle Thunder Prison.

But Mrs. Allan was one step ahead of Winder. By the time he returned to the Hoge home, she told him she'd obtained permission from the Sisters of Charity at St. Francis de Sales Asylum on Brook Avenue to stay there until her hearing. Winder consented. Around this same time, Winder had tracked down the man whom Mrs. Allan claimed had given the "Santa Trinita" letter to her servant. But it was a dead end.

Richmond was abuzz with rumor and innuendo—not to mention outrage. Not only had Mrs. Allan committed treason, they believed, but it seemed that her social position had spared her from the dark horrors of Castle Thunder. The *Examiner* fumed that Mrs. Allan had chosen to "prostitute [her] position to the basest of crimes" and didn't deserve special treatment. On top of that, Richmonders believed Mrs. Allan had betrayed her close friend Mrs. Hoge. One Richmond lady asserted that Mrs. Allan's "simulated sympathy" toward Mrs. Hoge during her difficulties was treachery "more fiendish than that to the government which she had affected to sustain by her sympathy, her wealth and her influence." The *Enquirer* agreed, saying, "In Dr. Hoge's family she had been treated with all kindness, and deserves to be branded after the manner practised by Philip of Macedon, 'the ungrateful guest.'"[197]

But that wasn't how Mrs. Hoge felt about the whole thing. She wrote to her husband in Europe, saying Mrs. Allan had *sent* the letters but didn't believe she *wrote* them.[198] Sending them wouldn't get Mrs. Allan in trouble with the Confederate government—that is, unless she was aware of their contents. In the coming weeks and months, the Hoge family would prove Mrs. Allan's staunchest allies.

Mrs. Allan's wealth afforded her two high-powered Richmond attorneys. One was James Lyons, who'd just served a term in the Confederate Congress, and the other was George W. Randolph, former Confederate secretary of war and grandson of Thomas Jefferson. Today, we'd call them a dream team.

Much to the consternation of Richmonders, there was a delay in bringing the accused in for questioning. The *Dispatch* said that Mrs. Allan was "confined to her bed" at the asylum, "threatened with brain fever," and the *Examiner* added that her head had "been shaved and a blister applied."[199] Her doctor was to make daily reports to General Winder on her condition. With the

Confederate government turning the screws on her, Mrs. Allan was suffering extreme emotional distress. "Her mental excitement will probably drive her to madness," said her surgeon. But the *Examiner* looked on the bright side, quipping, "The upshot of the business will probably be the return of Mrs. Patterson Allan to her original hogs in Cincinnati."[200]

In an atmosphere with zero tolerance for treason, some of the city's dailies took the liberty of saying that Mrs. Allan had actually written the letters. The public was hungrier than ever for details, so the papers tracked the case with painstaking detail. But there wasn't much to report until December 8, when General Winder formally charged Mrs. Allan with "treason in adhering to the enemies of the Confederate States, in giving them aid and comfort by writing and sending, or attempting to send, a letter of advice and intelligence to the enemy."

About a week later, a grand jury was finally convened. By that time, Reverend Hoge had returned to Richmond through the blockade, safe and sound.

———◦—◦———

In December 1863, five months after the treasonous letters surfaced, the hearings finally commenced. Officiating was Confederate States' Commissioner, William F. Watson. The prosecutor for the Confederate government was P.H. Aylett, a grandson of Patrick Henry.

The two-month-long hearings each opened with the same theatrical flourish. "Mrs. Allan, who was neatly attired in a plain black silk dress and closely veiled, entered the Court-room, leaning upon the arm of her husband," reported the *Dispatch* on December 16, "her counsel, Hon. James Lyons and Gen. George W. Randolph, arriving a few minutes afterwards." Throughout the proceedings, Mrs. Allan kept her thick veil down, "never revealing her features to the curious gaze of the spectators."[201] It seems there was a very *Perry Mason* feel to the whole interrogation.

The prosecutor presented a slew of testimony. He showed that Reverend Dix of New York—the man to whom the "Santa Trinita" letter had been addressed—was hardly a stranger to Mrs. Allan. They had been acquainted with each other in Italy, which could explain the "Caro Signore" reference in the letter. There was also testimony from William Burns—the man who discovered the letter—but the defense set out to impugn his reputation since he was a gambler. Further evidence revealed that during Stoneman's raid, Mrs. Allan had entertained Federal officers, who carefully spared her husband's property.

But Mrs. Allan's defense team came out swinging. For one thing, they presented several witnesses who attested to her Southern sympathies. One of the Hoge daughters testified that she had never heard Mrs. Allan express anything but "the most loyal sentiments towards the South." The defense also tried to show that Mrs. Allan couldn't possibly have betrayed Reverend Hoge. Mrs. Hoge testified that Mrs. Allan's "conduct had always been kind and affectionate to every member of the family, *more especially Mr. Hoge.*"

A major bone of contention was the handwriting on the intercepted letters. General Winder testified that his investigation proved the letters were in Mrs. Allan's handwriting. And another witness, the man who'd handed the letters to Burns, had known Mrs. Allan's handwriting for years—and testified that the treasonous letters were in her hand. But again, the Hoge family came to her defense. The Hoges' daughter testified she didn't see "the slightest resemblance between the chirography of the letter containing the treasonable matter and that of any other writing which she had seen of Mrs. Allan's."[202] Of course, the science of handwriting analysis wasn't nearly as advanced as it is today.

After all the testimony had been given, Mrs. Allan's lawyers presented her sworn affidavit of innocence:

> *This affiant doth solemnly declare upon her oath that she has never written or sent a letter to the Rev. Morgan Dix…and that she is not guilty of the charge now here alleged against her of having corresponded, or attempted to correspond, with him directly or indirectly, or of adhering to the enemies of the Confederate States, giving them aid and comfort.*
>
> *Mary Carolina Allan.*

Then James Lyons, counsel for the defense, made a final plea. He asked that Mrs. Allan be discharged since the evidence failed to prove that she wrote the "Santa Trinita" letter—or that she had any knowledge of its contents.

Then it was prosecutor Aylett's turn. According to the law, he said, all that mattered was whether there was *probable cause* to suspect Mrs. Allan of committing the offense.

Finally, seven months after the treasonous letters were discovered, it was the moment of truth. All eyes turned to Commissioner Watson as he rendered his decision. In part, he said:

In this case the accused is charged with treason in adhering to the enemies of the Confederate States of America, in giving them aid and comfort by writing and sending, or attempting to send, a letter of advice and intelligence to the enemies aforesaid, sometime during the month of June, 1863. That such a crime has been committed by some person; that such a letter was written and intended to be sent to the enemy, and was intercepted, the testimony establishes…The questions are, who wrote this letter? Who contemplated sending it to the enemy, having the knowledge of its contents? If there was not in the mind of the Court probable cause to implicate the accused in the charge against her, it would be my duty to discharge her. But that this letter came from her hands and was attempted to be communicated by her to the enemy, is proved by the testimony.

But did she write the letter? And if not, did she attempt to send it to the enemy, she having a knowledge of the contents? These are questions not for me to solve; for me there is developed in their attempted solution that probable cause of guilt, which impale [sic] me to send on the accused for final trial, and I accordingly commit her for that purpose.

Mrs. Allan was devastated and left the courtroom, "bitterly weeping."[203]

⇒•⟨⇐

The high treason trial of Mary Caroline Allan was scheduled to begin in March 1864. Pending trial, Judge James D. Halyburton freed her on $100,000 bond—a tremendous sum in those days. As Mrs. Allan retired to her luxurious home on the James River, Richmonders were more incensed than ever.

There were numerous delays in getting the trial underway. But they weren't due entirely to brilliant legal maneuvering, as has been suggested. One reason was the failing health of defense attorney George W. Randolph. Suffering with tuberculosis, he finally went to London in November 1864 to seek specialized medical attention. By February 1865, he was in France, completely debilitated.[204]

That same month, the editor of the *Dispatch* wrote a rambling piece about the highly publicized case. For far too long, he said, Richmonders had been barraged with accounts of the crime—and the $100,000 bail bond.

He added that:

it is a question whether, even with the aid of that amount, Mrs. Patterson Allan's best friend will be able to recognize her by the time her case is ended. Summers bloom and fade; and winters come and go; battles are fought; campaign follows campaign; great military reputations are born and die; well-known citizens are borne to their last home, and whole hosts of young soldiers vanish from the earth together, but "Mrs. Patterson Allan" never becomes extinct.—She is always appearing and disappearing, and we verily believe will continue to do the same till the present generation is gathered to its fathers. Girls who were born when that case was young will be married and become mothers before it is ended; boys will grow up, enter the army, and die on the field of honor, before we hear the last of "Mrs. Patterson Allan." We are not certain that peace itself may not arrive before the conclusion of that investigation. There are people who predict that the end of the world will occur in this century. We have heard no one venture a prediction of the end of the case of "Mrs. Patterson Allan." We are confident that the last paragraph which the youngest Confederate baby, who lives to become an octogenarian, will read in the newspapers will be this: "Mrs. Patterson Allan, recognized in the sum of one hundred thousand dollars for her appearance to answer an indictment for treason," etc.[205]

In a sense, that editor would prove right. Mrs. Allan's trial never took place. The Confederacy met its fateful end just two months later, rendering her case moot. She was soon freed.

⊰•◦•⊱

They say you're innocent until proven guilty. Yet today, some sources report that Mary Caroline Allan committed treason, and others report that she *allegedly* committed treason. One of the most caustic accounts was written by a Virginian the year after the fall of the Confederacy, while memories of the war were still fresh. Since Mrs. Allan was allowed to stay at an infirmary during her hearings, he fulminated, "for nearly six months the vulgarity of a legal prison was spared her, and a romantic confinement in a charitable institution was the chivalric invention of the Confederacy for the crime of treason!"[206]

We'll never know if Mrs. Allan wrote the letters or not. By the same token, we'll never know how she felt about the Union victory—whether she was devastated, or if she danced a gleeful jig.

Chapter 21

MIRACLE IN THE TRENCHES

Hungry Soldiers Offered a Bountiful Spread

By the middle of the war, sources of food were being choked off to a slow trickle. Much of what managed to get through was priced out of reach. Even the soldiers manning Richmond's Outer Defenses—near today's Martin's Grocery Store on Brook Road—practically starved to death. They probably would have given their right arm for some fried chicken, pecan pie tarts or even a cup of coffee.

Then, during Sheridan's Raid on Richmond in May 1864, while those men were "praying devoutly for something to eat," a miracle occurred. "A diminutive negro" was "making his way across wide, intervening fields from the direction of a thrifty farm house," the *Richmond Examiner* reported. He finally approached the man on picket duty.

"Missus says all you'ens of the company who are hungry, come over theer to her house," he exclaimed, pointing over the hill. "She has plenty to eat. Wanted the whole company to come."

A few lucky men were chosen to go first. "Never did men step with greater alacrity toward the goal of any desire," said the *Examiner*. As famished as they were, they ran. The first half dozen or so arrived at the friendly house first and met the lady who'd extended the invitation. She graciously invited them all in.

She said she'd prepared a little something for the hungry men, which she would "sell as low as the next one." Presenting a table spread with tempting delights, she ran over the rates attached to each. "There's ham and eggs, ten dollars. Pure coffee, five dollars per cup. Bread and butter, two dollars and a half. Nice sweet milk, one dollar a glass. What will you have, gentlemen?"

Several who had money jumped forward, but hearts sank for the others when they realized they weren't true guests after all.

The whole group slunk back to the entrenchments, and no more men were sent to the lady's house. They were repulsed by her stunt, the paper said, "and those who had been deceived into the run to her hospitable mansion were very anxious to be allowed the privilege of pitching a shell into it."

Chapter 22

CHESTER'S CAMPAIGN

Black War Correspondent Trumpets the End of Slavery

The river of blood would soon run dry.

In early April 1865, adrenaline-stoked Union troops closed in on the Confederate capital of Richmond. The red glow of fire in the sky signaled that Richmond had been evacuated. Over the coming hours and days, the scenes that unfolded were almost beyond words. At the center of every surreal moment was Thomas Morris Chester, a black war correspondent with the white newspaper, the *Philadelphia Press*. The first and only African American to report on the war for a major daily newspaper, his writings had a far different slant than Southern papers.

Writing under the pen name Rollin, Chester had quite a pedigree. A devout Unionist and son of a runaway slave, he had an abiding commitment to ending the oppression and exploitation of blacks. To that end, he'd been a prominent champion of Liberian colonization in the 1850s. After immigrating there himself, he launched and edited a newspaper, the *Star of Liberia*, and taught school at a new settlement. On hiatus in 1856, he was the only black student to graduate from Thetford Academy in Vermont, where he proved himself a skilled debater. And his recent reports from the front lines near Richmond and Petersburg had drawn attention to the devotion of the U.S. Colored Troops, whom he'd helped recruit in his home state of Pennsylvania.

With the capture of the Confederate capital eminent, Northerners were eager for Chester's eloquent, eyewitness accounts. On the other end of

Relishing the fall of Richmond was northern reporter Thomas Morris Chester, a longtime fighter against the oppression of blacks. *New York Public Library.*

the spectrum, upper-class Richmonders were crushed that their beloved city was about to fall into the hands of a despised enemy.

Just before dawn on April 3, Chester rode on horseback alongside the Union forces as they reached the eastern outskirts of the city. He describes being greeted with glee by blacks and poor whites:

The citizens stood gaping in wonder at the splendidly-equipped army marching along under the graceful folds of the old flag. Some waved their hats and women their hands in token of gladness. The pious old negroes, male and female, indulged in such expressions: "You've come at last"; "We've been looking for you these many days"; "Jesus has opened the way"; "God bless you"; "I've not seen that old flag for four years"; "It does my eyes good"; "Have you come to stay?"; "Thank God", and similar expressions of exultation. The soldiers, black and white, received these assurances of loyalty as evidences of the latent patriotism of an oppressed people, which a military despotism has not been able to crush.

As the victorious Union forces marched in formation into the city proper, "all the Government buildings were in flames," Chester reported, and "the flames soon communicated themselves to the business part of the city." Leading the forces were black troops of the Twenty-fifth Army Corps. Chester savored the irony. "There may be others," he said, "who may claim the distinction of being the first to enter the city, but as I was ahead of every

Chester swelled with pride as black Richmonders poured into the streets to welcome the first conquerors with the U.S. Colored Troops. *Library of Virginia.*

part of the force but the cavalry, which of necessity must lead the advance, I know whereof I affirm when I announce that General Draper's brigade [of Colored Troops] was the first organization to enter the city limits." Black Richmonders, free and slave, poured into the streets to welcome these first conquerors.

Around 8:15, Mayor Mayo formally surrendered the city to Union General Weitzel. The general and his staff then "rode up Main street amid the hearty congratulations of a very large crowd of colored persons and poor whites, who were gathered together upon the sidewalks manifesting every demonstration of joy."

Chester became wary when he observed that citizens "in the better-class houses" were "peeping out of the windows." He wondered if they'd cause trouble later. "There was no mistaking the curl of their lips and the flash of their eyes," he wrote.

As the raging fire continued to spread, its flames reaching high into the sky, Chester watched it engulf "poor and rich houses alike." The scene evoked his strong Union sympathies: "All classes were soon rushing, into the streets with their goods, to save them. They hardly laid them down before they were picked up by those who openly were plundering everyplace where anything of value was to be obtained. It was retributive justice upon the aiders and abettors of treason to see their property fired by the rebel chiefs and plundered by the people whom they meant to forever enslave."

In fact, plunder was the order of the day, as a mob sacked the stores on Main Street.

> *Men would rush to the principal stores, break open the doors, and carry off the contents by the armful. The leader of this system of public plundering was a colored man who carried upon his shoulder an iron crow-bar, and as a mark of distinguishment had a red piece of goods around his waist which reached down to his knees. The mob, for it could not with propriety be called anything else, followed him as their leader; moved on when he advanced, and rushed into every passage which was made by the leader with his crow-bar. Goods of every description were seized under these circumstances and personally appropriated by the supporters of an equal distribution of property. Cotton goods in abundance, tobacco in untold quantities, shoes, rebel military clothing, and goods and furniture generally were carried away by the people as long as any thing of value was to be obtained.*

After the worst of the fire was extinguished, things finally seemed under control. "Order once more reigns in Richmond," Chester wrote.

Meanwhile, imprisoned African Americans got the happiest of surprises. Chester described how "the jails in this place were thrown open, and all runaway negroes, those for sale and those for safe keeping were told to hop out and enjoy their freedom."

<hr />

Chester put all the aforementioned details into his dispatch of April 4, the day after Richmond came under Federal rule. He had made his way to the Capitol building, where the Confederate Congress formerly met. In his contempt for the Confederacy, he boldly sat down in the throne-like Speaker's chair, "so long dedicated to treason, but in the future to be consecrated to loyalty," and began writing. Chester didn't mention what happened next—it came to light by the *Boston Journal's* Charles C. Coffin and the *New York Tribune's* Charles A. Page. A paroled Confederate officer spied Chester, clenched his fist and shouted, "Come out of there, you black cuss!" Chester looked up, calmly eyed the officer and resumed his writing. "Get out of there, or I'll knock your brains out!" the officer bellowed. Then, uttering "a torrent of oaths," the officer charged at Chester and "laid hold of him to take him out." Tall and muscular, "Chester planted a black fist and left a black eye and a prostrate Rebel." Chester sat right back down to resume his dispatch, as if nothing had happened. Suddenly, the Confederate officer sprang to his feet and demanded the sword of a Union officer standing nearby, so he could "cut the damned nigger's heart out."

The Union officer replied, "Oh no, I guess not. I can't let you have my sword for any such purpose. If you want to fight, I will clear a space here, and see that you have fair play, but let me tell you that you will get a tremendous thrashing." The Confederate officer left the hall in disgust, and Chester went back to his writing.

The very day Chester ushered in a new order in Richmond, he documented another spectacle. President Lincoln arrived at Rocketts Wharf. The news spread, Chester said, "as if upon the wings of lightning, that 'Old Abe,' for it was treason in this city to give him a more respectful address, had come." Slaves greeted him with utter joy. Chester recounted Lincoln's walk to "Jeff Davis' house, the headquarters of General Weitzel," with a huge crowd following. After a thirty-minute meeting in the mansion, Lincoln was taken by carriage "through the principal streets." Chester was practically at a loss for words. "The colored population was wild with enthusiasm," he wrote. "Old men thanked God in a very boisterous manner, and old women shouted upon the pavement as high as they had ever done at a religious revival." Finally, the president's entourage arrived at Capital Square, which was packed with people. "Washington's monument and the Capitol steps were one mass of humanity to catch a glimpse of him," Chester reported.

He said Lincoln's visit presented a "spectacle of jubilee" unlike Richmond had ever seen:

> It must be confessed that those who participated in this informal reception of the President were mainly negroes. There were many whites in the crowd, but they were lost in the great concourse of American citizens of African descent. Those who lived in the finest houses either stood motionless upon their steps or merely peeped through the window-blinds, with a very few exceptions. The Secesh-inhabitants still have some hope for their tumbling cause.

As President Lincoln reached the former Confederate White House, thousands rushed in to catch a glimpse of him. *Library of Virginia.*

That evening, President Lincoln returned to Rocketts Wharf and boarded a cutter. As he pushed off, "amid the cheering of the crowd, another good old colored female shouted out, 'Don't drown, Massa Abe, for God's sake.'"

On Thursday, April 6, the newly freed slaves gathered for the jubilee of all jubilees. Chester himself called the meeting to order at the First African Church on Broad Street. It could normally seat one thousand people, but today twice that number squeezed in. Turning out "in full force" were black Richmonders and soldiers of the U.S. Colored Troops. "Every seat was taken up and all standing room was occupied," Chester observed, "the windows were thronged, and hundreds were outside unable to get within hearing or seeing distance." Chester proudly congratulated them on the "triumph of liberty in Richmond, and urged them, as redeemed freemen, to assume the

When Richmond fell, African Americans packed into the First African Church on Broad Street, where Chester hailed the "triumph of liberty in Richmond." *Library of Congress.*

duties and responsibilities belonging to the change." The crowd cheered him, as if to raise the roof. Giving the next speech was black chaplain David Stevens. History was made again. Richmond authorities had always required a white man to lead church gatherings, for fear that unsupervised negroes would organize an insurrection. One of the hymns smilingly sung that day was by Isaac Watts: "I'm going to join in this army/I'm going to join in this army of my Lord."

Three days later, on Sunday, April 9, Chester noted that Richmond businesses were beginning to reopen—that is, the ones surviving the fire. He observed that, "The excitement attending the occupation of this city by the Union army is gradually subsiding."

Church services were held that day, and again, the First African Church was "densely packed." The white pastor "preached a rebel sermon," Chester remarked, and "the colored soldiers…abruptly left the building." As the pastor exited the church, the black soldiers arrested him. Members of the congregation "begged and entreated that he might be spared the indignity of an arrest, out of respect to his age." But the pastor was forced to report to the provost marshal "to answer the charge of using improper language." The Federal government had outlawed any expression of Confederate sympathy.

The next morning came an ominous sign. Heavy artillery fire was "thundering around the city." Chester reported that loyal Confederates in Richmond "supposed that Lee, in accordance with the wishes of the rebels here, was making an effort to recapture this citadel of treason." But nothing could have been further from the truth. It was actually "salute after salute over the good news that Lee had surrendered, with the remnant of his badly whipped and demoralized forces," Chester explained. To him, the thunderous booms were poetic justice: "It was the funeral service over a God-forsaken Confederacy, with the artillery of the Union army and Porter's fleet, to chaunt [*sic*] the requiem." The citizens of Richmond, he predicted, "will soon learn that the rebellion is virtually at an end, and that freedom and the Union will hence forth maintain their supremacy over every inch of desecrated soil."

Later that morning, Chester overheard some Confederate officers state their willingness to take the oath of allegiance to the Union. But he didn't think they deserved the privileges of American citizenship. "Those who have forfeited that claim should be brought to a speedy and just punishment," he opined. "They refused, with scorn to heed the mercy of the Government; now let them experience its justice as a warning to treason in the future." Many Northerners bought in to Chester's argument.

———————

On April 15, Chester witnessed yet another event for the history books. As rain fell, the defeated General Lee entered Richmond. "The chieftain looked fatigued," Chester observed, "and rode along at a jaded gait…Several efforts were made to cheer him, which failed." His admirers quietly waved their hats and their hands. As Lee arrived at his home on Franklin Street, "he alighted from his horse" and "immediately uncovered his head, thinly covered with silver hairs." The small crowd pushed forward to shake hands with him. "Not a word was spoken," Chester said. The general bowed, ascended his steps and entered his house. Apparently, Chester had a certain degree of compassion for the Confederate chieftain. "The military authorities here will extend every consideration to Lee," he wrote.

The next day, around noon, Chester heard of "dreadful intelligence from Washington." President Lincoln had been assassinated. "The effect of this sad news has filled the heart of loyalty with mourning," Chester wrote. He claimed it even "caused the rebels to quake," since Lincoln's recent "conciliatory measures" had been "returned in a spirit of such fiendish barbarity." Then Chester expressed his personal grief, calling Lincoln "the great, the good, and the honest patriot."

That spring, Chester documented almost every aspect of Richmond's recovery, including the issuing of rations to the nearly starved citizens and the abolition of slavery.

He also denounced many injustices. In mid-May, Union officials instituted a pass system in Richmond for blacks. Soon thereafter, Joseph Mayo was reinstated as mayor along with his dreaded police force. Chester wrote that, "the good sense of the American people has been shocked by the elevation to trust and power of this old public sinner and his satellites whose treason in this city before the occupation was regarded as the standard for the Richmond rebels." Chester considered Mayo's reinstatement "little less than a crime." Two weeks after the pass system went into effect, eight hundred blacks had been arrested. There were numerous accounts of unnecessary assaults and intimidation.

Boldly, the black community fought back. A group wrote a letter to the *New York Tribune* on June 7, condemning the new pass system. "All that is needed to restore slavery in full," they railed, "is the auction block as it used to be." Local Union officials weren't willing to help, either. So, on June 10, over three thousand blacks held a public rally at the First African Church. A committee of ten was organized—including Chester—to plan an appeal to President Andrew Johnson.

Before the committee's seven-member delegation left for Washington, it presented evidence of extensive intimidation to Virginia governor Francis Pierpoint. He agreed to dismiss Mayo.

After arriving in Washington, the delegation was given an audience with President Johnson. They told him in their petition that they had earned the right to fair treatment, not the abuse the army was according them. In turn, he committed himself "to do all in his power to protect them and their rights."

At long, long last, Richmond was relinquished from the insanities of war and the blight of slavery. Yet the city's blacks faced generations of bitter struggle. Unfortunately, they'd have to find their way without the veteran rebel for their cause, Thomas Morris Chester. He left Richmond in July 1865 and returned to his home state of Pennsylvania.

In the coming decades, Chester built on his incredible successes. He became the European agent for a freedmen's aid society. He studied law in London and became the first black American to be admitted to the bar in England and, later, the state of Louisiana. And he was appointed brigadier general of the Louisiana militia.

So, while monuments were erected throughout the South to honor Confederates, Chester served as a beacon of hope for his race.

Notes

Chapter 1: Disaster on Brown's Island

1. *Richmond Examiner*, "Terrible Explosion on Brown's Island," March 14, 1863.
2. *Richmond Enquirer*, "Terrible Explosion," March 14, 1863.
3. *Richmond Examiner*, "Terrible Explosion on Brown's Island," March 14, 1863.
4. Ibid.
5. *Richmond Sentinel*, as quoted by David L. Burton in "Friday the 13th: Richmond's Great Homefront Disaster."

Chapter 2: Police Raid at Midnight

6. Lowry, *Sex in the Civil War*, 70.
7. DeLeon, *Four Years*, 238.
8. Ibid.
9. O'Connor, *Wanderings of a Vagabond*, 107.
10. *Richmond Whig*, "The Grog Shops and the Police—Reform Needed," July 1, 1864.
11. Chafetz, *Play the Devil*, 255.
12. Evans, *Judah P. Benjamin*, 219.

13. *Richmond Dispatch*, "The Gaming Cases," December 14, 1861.
14. *Richmond Dispatch*, "Descent Upon Fashionable Gambling Houses," November 11, 1861.
15. Ibid.
16. *Richmond Dispatch*, "A New Issue," November 25, 1861.
17. *Richmond Dispatch*, "The Gaming Cases," December 14, 1861.
18. *Richmond Dispatch*, "Hustings Court," December 17, 1861.
19. *Richmond Dispatch*, "The Law and the Faro Banks," December 16, 1861.
20. *Richmond Dispatch*, "Unlawful Gaming," October 22, 1863.
21. *Richmond Dispatch*, "Gaming House," November 12, 1863.
22. *New York Times*, "News from the Rebels," August 13, 1861.

CHAPTER 3: EYE IN THE SKY

23. *New York Times*, "Prof. Lowe and His Balloon," September 10, 1860.
24. *Richmond Dispatch*, "Balloons," May 27, 1861.
25. *Richmond Dispatch*, "Northern Military Affairs—Speculations on Southern Movements," June 21, 1861.
26. *Richmond Dispatch*, "Army Balloons," July 6, 1861.
27. *Richmond Dispatch*, "—— of the War," July 12, 1861.
28. *Richmond Enquirer*, "More Balloons," May 28, 1862.

CHAPTER 4: "THE LION"

29. *Richmond Dispatch*, "Candidates for Office," January 31, 1862.
30. Lyons, *Four Essays on Secession*.
31. DeLeon, *Four Years*, 129–30.
32. *Richmond Dispatch*, "Candidates for Office," January 31, 1862.
33. *Richmond Dispatch*, "Local Matters," January 17, 1862.
34. *Richmond Dispatch*, "To the People of the Country," July 27, 1861.
35. *Richmond Dispatch*, "James Lyons Esq." January 23, 1862.
36. *Richmond Dispatch*, "Candidates for Office," January 31, 1862.
37. Yearns, *The Confederate Congress*, 46.
38. Jones, *The Davis Memorial Volume*, 819.
39. Davis, *Jefferson Davis*, 206.

40. *Richmond Dispatch*, "Three Hundred Dollars Reward," June 25, 1863.

41. Hattaway and Beringer, *Jefferson Davis, Confederate President*, 191.

42. *Richmond Dispatch*, "For Governor," March 7, 1863.

43. *Richmond Dispatch*, "The Henrico Homicide—Preliminary Examination of Joseph Bernard, for the Murder of John O. Taylor," January 31, 1861; *Richmond Dispatch*, "Examination of Mrs. Patterson Allan," February 20, 1864; *Richmond Dispatch*, "Called Court," February 7, 1862.

44. *Richmond Dispatch*, "The Meeting for the Relief of Maimed Soldiers," January 27, 1864.

45. *Brief Review of the Plan and Operations of the Association for the Relief of Maimed Soldiers*. N.p., 1865.

46. *Richmond Dispatch*, "The Raid Around Richmond—Capture of Parties of the Enemy—The Fighting on the Brook Road and on Green's Farm," March 3, 1864; Henrico County Deeds, Book 100 (1877), 330–32.

47. Map of the defenses of Richmond & Petersburg. *Official Records Atlas*, Plate C, #2, 1865.

48. Howard, "Brig. Gen. Walter H. Stevens," 249.

49. Moore, *The Rebellion Record*, 584.

50. Report of Colonel Walter H. Stevens, C.S. Army, commanding Richmond defenses. March 8, 1864. *War of the Rebellion: A Compilation of the Official Records of the Union and Confederate Armies*, Vol. XXXIII. Washington: Government Printing Office, 1891, 212–13.

51. *Richmond Dispatch*, "Destructive Fire," March 17, 1864.

52. Ibid.

53. Harrison, "The Capture of Jefferson Davis," 131.

54. Jordan, *Black Confederates and Afro-Yankees in Civil War Virginia*, 235.

55. A.A. and Mary Hoeling, *The Last Days Of The Confederacy*, 139.

56. Pryor, *Reminiscences of Peace and War*, 355.

57. Wixson, ed., *From Civility to Survival*, 98.

58. Avary, *Dixie After the War*, 15–16.

59. *Times-Dispatch*, "Why Jefferson Davis Was Never Tried," February 19, 1911.

60. DeLeon, *Belles, Beaux and Brains of the Sixties*, 130.

CHAPTER 5: BLOODY CARAVAN FROM SEVEN PINES

61. *Richmond Dispatch*, "Obituaries," July 5, 1862; *Richmond Whig*, "The Hospitals," June 4, 1862.

CHAPTER 6: VIOLET'S WAR

62. Henrico County Deeds, Book 100 (1877), 330–32.
63. Map of the defenses of Richmond & Petersburg, from the Official Records Atlas, Plate C, #2. Prepared by Nathaniel Micheler, 1865.
64. *Richmond Dispatch*, "The Henrico Homicide," January 31, 1861.
65. *Richmond Dispatch*, "Death of Mr. Taylor," January 29, 1861.
66. *Richmond Dispatch*, "The Henrico Homicide," January 31, 1861.
67. Crist, ed., *The Papers of Jefferson Davis*, 195.
68. *Richmond Dispatch*, "Proceedings in the Courts," November 1, 1862.
69. *Richmond Dispatch*, "Notice.—Horses, Mules, Cows, Hogs, Household and Kitchen Furniture, Buggies, &c., at Public Auction," February 23, 1861.
70. *Richmond Dispatch*, "Twenty Five Dollar Reward," March 30, 1863.
71. *Richmond Dispatch*, "The Raid around Richmond," March 3, 1864.
72. Moore, *The Rebellion Record*, 584.
73. *Richmond Dispatch*, "The Raid around Richmond," March 3, 1864.

CHAPTER 7: CHEERS AT THE RICHMOND THEATRE

74. *Richmond Dispatch*, "Patriotism Exhibited Tangibly," December 3, 1861.
75. *Washington Post*, "Aged Actress Dies," January 12, 1907.
76. *Times-Dispatch*, "Death of Colonel George W. Alexander," March 3, 1895.
77. Ibid.
78. *Times-Dispatch*, "Old Castle Thunder," March 3, 1895.
79. Ibid.
80. Furgurson, *Ashes of Glory*, 235–36.
81. Henley, "Colonel George W. Alexander," 50.
82. Moore, *The Rebellion Record*, 24.
83. *Times-Dispatch*, "Sallie Partington—A Favorite of Theatregoers during Civil War Era," August 4, 1935.
84. *Times-Dispatch*, "Famous Actress Passes Beyond," January 12, 1907.
85. *Richmond Whig*, "That Big Black Dog," May 1, 1865.
86. Beymer, *Scouts and Spies of the Civil War*, 138.
87. *Times-Dispatch*, "Old Castle Thunder," March 3, 1895.

CHAPTER 8: CAMP LEE

88. *New York Times*, "Union Agricultural Fair at Richmond. &c," October 26, 1860.
89. *New York Times*, "Newspaper Indications," November 10, 1860.
90. *Richmond Dispatch*, "The Encampment," October 31, 1860.
91. *Richmond Dispatch*, "Camp Lee," October 30, 1860.
92. *Richmond Dispatch*, "The Presidential Election," November 8, 1860.
93. *Richmond Dispatch*, "Scenes at Camp Lee," November 9, 1860.
94. *Richmond Dispatch*, "Camp Lee," November 10, 1860.
95. *Richmond Enquirer*, "Volunteer Companies," April 27, 1861.
96. *Richmond Enquirer*, "Camp of Instruction at the Central Fair Grounds," April 27, 1861; *Richmond Dispatch*, "Regimental Order," April 29, 1861.
97. *Richmond Whig*, "Camp Lee," August 12, 1862.
98. *Richmond Dispatch*, "Sick Soldiers," April 30, 1861.
99. *Richmond Whig*, "Camp Lee," August 12, 1862.
100. *Richmond Whig*, "The Fair Grounds," May 22, 1861.
101. "Rev. Moses D. Hoge," *Confederate Veteran Magazine* 3, no. 2 (1895): 66–67.
102. *Richmond Enquirer*, May 30, 1861; Davis, *The Man and His Hour*, 338; *Richmond Dispatch*, "Arrival of President Davis," May 30, 1861.
103. Lonn, *Foreigners in the Confederacy*, 213.
104. *Richmond Dispatch*, "Trial, Sentence, and Execution of Timothy Webster as a Spy," April 30, 1862.
105. *Richmond Whig*, "Iron Clads Captured," April 29, 1864.
106. "Virginia's Contribution to the Confederacy," 141–42.
107. *The War of the Rebellion*, 1078.
108. *Papers of the Military Historical Society of Massachusetts*, 140.
109. "Camp Lee and the Freedmen's Bureau," 346–55.
110. "The Suburban Resorts Around and in Richmond—A Swing Around the Circle." *Southern Opinion*, June 27, 1867.

CHAPTER 9: THE MORDECAI LADIES

111. Beale, *A Lieutenant of Cavalry in Lee's Army*, 33; Wert, *Cavalryman of the Lost Cause*, 94; Joseph Bryan Park Historic Nomination Document.
112. *Richmond Dispatch*, "Steeple Blown Down," May 12, 1864.
113. Hartley, *Stuart's Tarheels*, 227.

CHAPTER 10. COPING WITHOUT COFFEE

114. Eggleston, "The Bride of '61," 162–63.
115. *Richmond Dispatch*, "Coffee," November 30, 1861.
116. *Natchez (MS) Daily Courier*, "Cotton Seed Coffee," February 7, 1862.
117. *Savannah Republican*, "Practical Hints for Hard Times," November 27, 1862.
118. Coulter, *Confederate States of America*, 245.
119. *Montgomery Weekly Advertiser*, "Okra Coffee," September 23, 1863.
120. *Richmond Dispatch*, Ad for Confederate Mills, February 10, 1862.
121. *Richmond Dispatch*, "Destruction by Fire of the Confederate Coffee Factory," February 24, 1864.
122. *Richmond Sentinel*, "Destructive Fire," February 24, 1864.
123. *Richmond Dispatch*, "Destruction by Fire of the Confederate Coffee Factory," February 24, 1864.
124. *Richmond Enquirer*, "Martial Law Over Richmond—Arrest of Hon. John Minor Botts and Other Suspected Unionists," March 4, 1862.
125. *Richmond Enquirer*, "Mr. Franklin Stearns," April 26, 1862.
126. *Richmond Sentinel*, "Destructive Fire," February 24, 1864.

CHAPTER 11. BORN FIGHTER, MARY EDWARDS WALKER

127. *Richmond Whig*, "Female Yankee Surgeon," April 22, 1864.
128. *Richmond Examiner*, "Miss Walker, The Yankee Surgeoness," June 29, 1864.
129. *Richmond Dispatch*, "Departures by Flag-of-truce," August 13, 1864.
130. *New York Times*, "Police Trials," June 14, 1866.

CHAPTER 12. MOONLIGHT COUNTERFEITERS

131. *Richmond Dispatch*, "Sentenced to Death," April 7, 1862.
132. *Richmond Dispatch*, "To Be Executed," August 14, 1862.
133. *Richmond Dispatch*, "Execution of a Counterfeiter," August 23, 1862.
134. *Richmond Dispatch*, "Arrest of an Alleged Counterfeiter," March 31, 1863.
135. *Richmond Dispatch*, "Hustings Court," November 12, 1863.
136. *Richmond Dispatch*, "Local Matters," February 9, 1865.
137. *Richmond Dispatch*, editor's column, February 17, 1865.

CHAPTER 13. THE BROOK CHURCH FIGHT

138. Poindexter, *An Illustrated History of Bryan Park*, 4.
139. *Journal of the Sixtieth Annual Convention of the Protestant Episcopal Church in Virginia.*, 91–92.
140. Cooke, ed., *Surry of Eagle's-nest*, 19.
141. Jones, *Life and Letters of Robert Edward Lee*, 438.
142. Hartley, *Stuart's Tarheels*, 2.
143. *Richmond Examiner*, "Death of General Gordon," May 20, 1864.
144. Diary of Emma Mordecai, 14.
145. Moore, ed., *The Rebellion Record*, Vol. 11, 459.
146. *Richmond Dispatch*, "A Church Burnt," August 3, 1864; Hartley, *Stuart's Tarheels*, 421.

CHAPTER 14. FOREIGN ASSISTANCE

147. Eaton, *History of the Southern Confederacy*, 217.
148. Gordon, "Hard Times in the Confederacy," 765.
149. *Richmond Dispatch*, "In Press," February 6, 1863.
150. Cooke, *Mohun*, 325.
151. *Richmond Whig*, "Lee's Miserables," June 12, 1863.

CHAPTER 15. RICHMOND'S QUEEN OF HOSPITALITY

152. Gouverneur, *As I Remember*, 63–64.
153. Wilson, *Thackeray in the United States*, 255.
154. DeLeon, *Belles, Beaux and Brains*, 198.
155. Ibid.
156. Tyler, "The Westmoreland Club in the History of Richmond from Its Building to the Present Day."
157. DeLeon, *Belles, Beaux and Brains*, 198.
158. Tyler, "The Westmoreland Club in the History of Richmond From Its Building to the Present Day."
159. DeLeon, *Belles, Beaux and Brains*, 200.
160. Meade, *Judah P. Benjamin*, 278.

161. *Richmond Dispatch*, "From Petersburg," July 2, 1861.
162. *Southern Historical Society Papers*, 421.
163. Patton, *Poems of John R. Thompson*, lviii.
164. Ibid, xix.
165. http://mshistorynow.mdah.state.ms.us/articles/173/lucius-quintus-cincinnatus-lamar, accessed 12/22/12.
166. Woodward, *Mary Chesnut's Civil War*, 428.
167. Ibid., 503.
168. Morgan, "The Lost Cause," 501.
169. DeLeon, *Belles, Beaux and Brains*, 199.
170. Settles, *John Bankhead Magruder*.
171. Ellet, *Queens of American Society*, 421.

CHAPTER 16. THE DREADED WHIPPING POST

172. Jordan, *Black Confederates and Afro-Yankees*, 157.
173. *Richmond Dispatch*, November 1, 27 and 29, 1860.
174. *Richmond Dispatch*, "Mayor's Court," March 19, 1861.
175. *Richmond Dispatch*, September 6, 1862; December 16, 1862; February 4, 1863.
176. *Richmond Dispatch*, "Martial law," March 12, 1862.
177. http://www.vahistorical.org/sva2003/post.htm, accessed January 5, 2013.

CHAPTER 17. FANFARE AT ROCKETTS WHARF

178. *Richmond Dispatch*, "Arrival of Confederate Prisoners," May 2, 1864.
179. Ibid.

CHAPTER 18. BECKMAN'S SALOON DOWN ON MAIN

180. *Richmond Dispatch*, "Lager Beer," July 1, 1863.
181. *Richmond Dispatch*, "A Tin Scrape," January 16, 1864.

182. *Richmond Dispatch*, May 6, 1863; May 7, 1863; February 19, 1863; June 4, 1863.

183. *Richmond Examiner*, "At the Castle," June 9, 1864.

CHAPTER 19. GEORGE ARENTS AND THE LINCOLN CONSPIRACY

184. *Richmond Dispatch*, "The Crisis—Its Commercial Aspect," January 26, 1861.

185. *Confederate Papers Relating to Citizens or Business Firms, 1861–65*. Record Group 109, Roll 0354. National Archives.

186. *Richmond Enquirer*, July 25, 1861.

187. *Compiled Service Records of Confederate Soldiers who served in organizations from the State of Virginia*, Reels 15, 213, 364. Library of Virginia; *Richmond Dispatch*, "Confederate States District Court," August 17, 1864; *Richmond Dispatch*, "Confederate States District Court," August 24, 1864.

188. Personal Property Tax Books, City of Richmond, 1862, pt. 3, Reel 829, Image 164. Library of Virginia.

189. *Richmond Examiner*, September 29, 1862.

190. *Richmond Dispatch*, April 13, June 15, September 14, October 12, 1863.

191. Hawley, *History of the Conspiracy*, 58.

192. *New York Times*, "Arents Left $10,040,643," October 29, 1918.

CHAPTER 20. AVENGING THE "TRAITORESS"

193. *Richmond Dispatch*, "Examination of Mrs. Patterson Allan," December 18, 1863.

194. *Richmond Examiner*, as referenced in the *Weekly Columbus (Ga.) Enquirer*, July 28, 1863.

195. *Richmond Dispatch*, "C.S. Commissioner's Court—Examination of Mrs. Patterson Allan Continued," December 19, 1863.

196. *Richmond Dispatch*, "Examination of Mrs. Patterson Allan, continued," December 21, 1863.

197. *Richmond Enquirer*, as referenced in the *Evening News* (Providence), July 28, 1863.

198. Furgurson, *Ashes of Glory*, 219.

199. *Richmond Dispatch*, "An Explanation," July 25, 1863; *Richmond Examiner*, as referenced in the *Weekly Columbus (Ga.) Enquirer*, July 28, 1863.

200. *Richmond Examiner*, as referenced in the *Evening News* (Providence) July 28, 1863.

201. *Richmond Dispatch*, December 16, 19, 1863.

202. *Richmond Dispatch*, December 18, 21, 1863.

203. *Richmond Dispatch*, "Examination of Mrs. Patterson Allan," February 20, 1864.

204. *Richmond Dispatch*, "Local Matters," February 9, 1865; Welsh, *Medical Histories of Confederate Generals*, 181.

205. *Richmond Dispatch*, editor's column, February 17, 1865.

206. Pollard, *Southern History of the War*, 201.

Bibliography

Chapter 1: Disaster on Brown's Island

Burton, David L. "Friday the 13th: Richmond's Great Home Front Disaster." *Civil War Times Illustrated* 21, no. 6 (October 1982): 36–41.

Richmond Enquirer.

Richmond Examiner.

Trowbridge, John T. *The South: A Tour of its Battle-fields and Ruined Cities.* Hartford, CT: L. Steebins, 1866, 153–205.

Chapter 2: Police Raid at Midnight

Acts of the General Assembly of the State of Virginia, Passed at Called Session, 1863, in the Eighty-Eighth Year of the Commonwealth. Richmond: William F. Ritchie, Public Printer, 1863.

Chafetz, Henry. *Play the Devil: A History of Gambling in the United States from 1492 to 1955.* New York: Clarkson N. Potter, Inc., 1960.

Coffin, Charles Carleton. *Drum-Beat of the Nation.* New York: Harper & Brothers, 1915.

DeLeon, T.C. *Four Years in Rebel Capitals*. Mobile, AL: Gossip Printing Co., 1890.

Evans, Eli N. *Judah P. Benjamin: The Jewish Confederate*. New York: Free Press, 1988.

Lowry, Thomas P., MD. *The Story the Soldiers Wouldn't Tell: Sex in the Civil War*. Mechanicsville, PA: Stackpole Books, 1994.

New York Times.

O'Connor, John. *Wanderings of a Vagabond: An Autobiography*. New York: self-published, 1873.

Rhodes, James Ford. *History of the United States*, Vol. 5. New York: MacMillan Company, 1906.

Richmond Dispatch.

Richmond Whig.

Thomas, Emory M. *The Confederate State of Richmond*. Baton Rouge: Louisiana State University Press, 2008.

CHAPTER 3: EYE IN THE SKY

The Aero Club of America. *Navigating the Air*. London: William Heinemann, 1907.

Evans, Charles M. *War of the Aeronauts: A History of Ballooning in the Civil War*. Mechanicsburg, PA: Stackpole Books, 2002.

New York Times.

"Our March Against Pope." In *Battles and Leaders of the Civil War*. Vol. 2. Secaucus, NJ: Castle, n.d.

Quarstein, John V. *The Monitor Boys: The Crew of the Union's First Ironclad*. Charleston, SC: The History Press, 2011.

Richmond Dispatch.

Richmond Enquirer.

Wagner, Margaret E., Gary W. Gallagher, Paul Finkelman. *The Library of Congress Civil War Desk Reference*. New York: Simon and Schuster, 2002.

CHAPTER 4: "THE LION"

Alexander, Ann Field. *Race Man: The Rise and Fall of the "Fighting Editor," John Mitchell, Jr*. Charlottesville: University of Virginia Press, 2002.

Avary, Myrta Lockett. *Dixie After the War.* New York: Doubleday, Page & Co., 1906.

Bridges, Peter. *Pen of Fire: John Moncure Daniel.* Kent, OH: Kent State University Press, 2002.

Brief Review of the Plan and Operations of the Association for the Relief of Maimed Soldiers. N.p., 1865.

Davis, Varina Howell. *Jefferson Davis, Ex-President of the Confederate States of America,* Vol. 2. New York: Belford Company, 1890.

DeLeon, T.C. *Four Years in Rebel Capitals.* Mobile, AL: Gossip Printing Co., 1890.

DeLeon, Thomas C. *Belles, Beaux and Brains of the Sixties.* New York: G.W. Dillingham Co., 1909.

"Foreign Recognition of the Confederacy—Letter from Honorable James Lyons." *Southern Historical Society Papers,* Vol. 7. Broadfoot Publishing Co., 1878.

Harrison, Burton N. "The Capture of Jefferson Davis," *The Century Illustrated Monthly Magazine* 27 (1884): 130–145.

Hattaway, Herman, and Richard E. Beringer. *Jefferson Davis, Confederate President.* Lawrence: University Press of Kansas, 2002.

Henrico County Deeds, Book 100 (1887): 330–32.

Hoeling, A.A. and Mary. *The Last Days Of The Confederacy.* New York: Fairfax Press, 1981.

Howard, James McH. "Brig. Gen. Walter H. Stevens." *The Confederate Veteran Magazine* 30 (1922): 249.

Jones, J. Wm. *The Davis Memorial Volume.* Richmond: B.F. Johnson & Co., 1890.

Jones, John Beauchamp. *A Rebel War Clerk's Diary at the Confederate States Capital,* Vol. 2. Philadelphia: J.B. Lippincott & Co., 1866.

Jordan, Ervin L. *Black Confederates and Afro-Yankees in Civil War Virginia.* Charlottesville: University Press of Virginia, 1995.

Lyons, James. "Four Essays on the Right and Propriety of Secession by Southern States." Richmond: Ritchie & Dunnavant, 1861.

Map of the Defenses of Richmond & Petersburg. *Official Records Atlas,* plate C, no. 2, 1865.

Moore, Frank, ed., *The Rebellion Record,* Vol. 8. New York: D. Van Nostrand, 1865.

Pollard, Edward Alfred. *Southern History of the War.* New York: C.B. Richardson, 1865.

Pryor, Mrs. Roger A. *Reminiscences of Peace and War.* New York: The Macmillan Company, 1904.

Report of Colonel Walter H. Stevens, C.S. Army, commanding Richmond defenses, March 8, 1864. *War of the Rebellion: A Compilation of the Official*

Records of the Union and Confederate Armies, Vol. XXXIII. Washington, D.C.: Government Printing Office, 1891.

Richmond Dispatch.

Richmond Times-Dispatch.

Strode, Hudson. *Jefferson Davis: Confederate President.* New York: Harcourt, Brace and Company, 1959.

————. *Jefferson Davis: Tragic Hero.* New York: Harcourt, Brace & World, Inc., 1964.

Thomas, Emory M. *The Confederate State of Richmond.* Baton Rouge: Louisiana State University Press, 2008.

Tyler, Alice M. "The Westmoreland Club in the History of Richmond From Its Building to the Present Day." *Richmond Times-Dispatch,* June 9, 1912.

Wixson, Neal E., ed. *From Civility to Survival: Richmond Ladies During the Civil War.* Bloomington, IN: iUniverse, 2012.

Yearns, Wilfred Buck. *The Confederate Congress.* Athens: University of Georgia Press, 2010.

CHAPTER 5: BLOODY CARAVAN FROM SEVEN PINES

Battles and Leaders of the Civil War, Vol. 2. Secaucus, NJ: Castle, n.d.

Calcutt, Rebecca Barbour. *Richmond's Wartime Hospitals.* Gretna, LA: Pelican Publishing, 2005.

Dictionary of North Carolina Biography, Vol. 5. Chapel Hill: University of North Carolina Press, 1994.

Hamilton, J.G. de Roulhac, and Rebecca Cameron, eds. *The Papers of Randolph Abbott Shotwell,* Vol. 1. Raleigh: North Carolina Historical Commission, 1929.

McCaslin, Richard B. *A Photographic History of North Carolina in the Civil War.* Fayetteville: University of Arkansas Press, 1997.

"Other Southern Subjects." *Virginia Cavalcade* 42, no. 1 (1992).

Richmond Dispatch.

Richmond Whig.

Thomas, Emory M. *The Confederate State of Richmond.* Baton Rouge: Louisiana State University Press, 2008.

Wixson, Neal E. *From Civility to Survival: Richmond Ladies During the Civil War.* Bloomington, ID: iUniverse, 2012.

CHAPTER 6: VIOLET'S WAR

Crist, Lynda Lasswell, ed. *The Papers of Jefferson Davis: 1861*, Vol. 7. Baton Rouge: Louisiana State University Press, 1992.

Henrico County Deeds, Book 100 (1877): 330–32.

Map of the Defenses of Richmond & Petersburg. *Official Records Atlas*, plate C, no. 2. Prepared by Nathaniel Micheler, 1865.

Moore, Frank, ed. *The Rebellion Record*, Vol. 8. New York: D. Van Nostrand, 1865.

Richmond Dispatch.

The Virginia Law Register, Vol. 14. Charlottesville: Michie Company, 1909.

CHAPTER 7: CHEERS AT THE RICHMOND THEATRE

Beymer, William Gilmore. *Scouts and Spies of the Civil War.* Lincoln: University of Nebraska Press, 1912.

Casstevens, Frances H. *George W. Alexander and Castle Thunder: A Confederate Prison and Its Commandant.* Jefferson, NC: Macfarland & Co., Inc., 2004.

Confederate States of America, Committee to Enquire into the Treatment of Prisoners at Castle Thunder. Evidence Taken Before the Committee of the House of Representatives, Appointed to Enquire Into the Treatment of Prisoners at Castle Thunder. N.p., 1863.

Davis, William C., and James I. Roberson, Jr., eds. *Virginia at War, 1865.* Lexington: University Press of Kentucky, 2012.

Furgurson, Ernest B. *Ashes of Glory.* New York: Alfred A. Knopf, 1997.

Goss, Warren Lee. *The Soldier's Story of his Captivity at Andersonville, Belle Island, and Other Rebel Prisons.* Scituate, MA: Digital Scanning, Inc., 2001.

Heidler, David Stephen, Jeanne T. Heidler, David J. Coles. *Encyclopedia of the American Civil War: A Political, Social, and Military History.* New York: W.W. Norton & Company, 2002.

Henley, Bernard John. "Colonel George W. Alexander: the Terror of Castle Thunder." *The Richmond Literature and History Quarterly* 3, no. 2 (Fall 1980).

Moore, Frank, ed. *The Rebellion Record*, Vol. 8. New York: D. Van Nostrand, 1865.

Richmond Dispatch.

Richmond Times-Dispatch.

Richmond Whig.

Thomas, Emory M. *The Confederate State of Richmond.* Baton Rouge: Louisiana State University Press, 1998.

Velazquez, Loreta Janeta. *The Woman In Battle.* Richmond: Dustin, Gilman & Co., 1876.

Washington Post.

Washington Times. "Rebel Raider Disguised in Hoop Skirt." October 6, 2007.

Chapter 8: Camp Lee

Civil War Times Illustrated 2, no. 6 (October 1963): 7.

Cooke, John Esten. *Stonewall Jackson: A Military Biography.* New York: D. Appleton & Co., 1876.

Davis, William C. *Jefferson Davis: The Man and His Hour.* Baton Rouge: Louisiana State University Press, 1996.

Furgurson, Ernest B. *Ashes of Glory.* New York: Alfred A. Knopf, 1997.

Fitzhugh, George. "Camp Lee." *The Old Guard* 3, no. 12 (December 1865): 533–65.

———. "Camp Lee and the Freedman's Bureau." *Debow's Review, Agricultural, Commercial, Industrial Progress and Resources* 2, no. 4 (October 1866): 346–55.

Gatewood, Andrew C. L., Papers, Manuscript #068. VMI Archives.

Hoge, Peyton Harrison. *Moses Drury Hoge: Life and Letters.* Richmond: Whittet & Shepperson, 1899.

Kimmel, Stanley. *Mr. Davis's Richmond.* New York: Coward-McCann, Inc., 1958.

Lonn, Ella. *Foreigners in the Confederacy.* Chapel Hill: University of North Carolina Press Books, 2002.

New York Times.

Official Website for Virginia Military Institute. http://www.vmi.edu.

Papers of the Military Historical Society of Massachusetts, Volume 14. Boston: Military Historical Society of Massachusetts, 1918.

"Rev. Moses D. Hoge." *Confederate Veteran Magazine* 3, no. 2 (1895).

Richmond Dispatch.

Richmond Enquirer.

Richmond Whig.

Robertson, James I., Jr. *Stonewall Jackson: The Man, The Soldier, The Legend.* New York: Simon & Schuster Macmillan, 1997.

Shields, John C. "The Old Camp Lee." Reprinted from *Richmond Dispatch,* May 22, 1898. *Southern Historical Society Papers* 26 (1898).

"The Suburban Resorts Around and in Richmond—A Swing Around the Circle." *Southern Opinion,* June 27, 1867.

"Virginia's Contribution to the Confederacy." *William and Mary College Quarterly Historical Magazine* 13, no. 2 (October 1904).

The War of the Rebellion series 1, vol. 46, part 3. Washington, D.C.: Government Printing Office, 1894.

CHAPTER 9: THE MORDECAI LADIES

Beale, George William. *A Lieutenant of Cavalry in Lee's Army.* Boston: Gorham Press, 1918.

Bingham, Emily. *Mordecai: An Early American Family.* New York: Hill and Wang, 2003.

Hartley, Chris J. *Stuart's Tarheels.* Jefferson, NC: McFarland & Co., Inc., 2011.

Mordecai, Emma. Diary, May 1864–May 1865. Typescript copy, Virginia Historical Society.

Poindexter, G.W. *An Illustrated History of Joseph Bryan Park.* Richmond: B&B Printing, 2003.

Richmond Dispatch.

Virginia Department of Historic Resources. *Joseph Bryan Park Historic Nomination Document,* 2002.

Wert, Jeffry D. *Cavalryman of the Lost Cause: A Biography of J.E.B. Stuart.* New York: Simon and Schuster, 2009.

CHAPTER 10: COPING WITHOUT COFFEE

Christian, W. Asbury. *Richmond: Her Past and Present.* Richmond: L.H. Jenkins, 1912.

Coulter, E. Merton. *The Confederate States of America, 1861–1865,* Vol. 7. Baton Rouge: Louisiana State University Press, 1950.

Eggleston, Sarah D. "The Bride of '61," In *Our Women In The War* (Charleston, SC: News and Courier, 1885), 162–63.

Montgomery Weekly Advertiser.

Natchez (MS) Daily Courier.

Richmond Dispatch.

Richmond Enquirer.
Richmond Sentinel.
Savannah Republican.
Schwab, John Christopher. *The Confederate States of America, 1861–1865: A Financial and Industrial History of the South During the Civil War.* New York: Charles Scribner's Sons, 1901.

CHAPTER 11: BORN FIGHTER, MARY EDWARDS WALKER

New York Times.
Richmond Dispatch.
Richmond Examiner.
Richmond Whig.
Walker, Dale L. *Mary Edwards Walker: Above and Beyond.* New York: Tom Dogerty Associates, LLC, 2005.

CHAPTER 12: MOONLIGHT COUNTERFEITERS

Benner, Judith Ann. *Fraudulent Finance: Counterfeiting and the Confederate States, 1861–1865.* Hillsboro, TX: Hill Junior College Press, 1970.
Buhk, Tobin T. *True Crime in the Civil War.* Mechanicsville, PA: Stackpole Books, 2012.
Richmond Dispatch.

CHAPTER 13: THE BROOK CHURCH FIGHT

Cooke, John Esten, ed. *Surry of Eagle's-nest.* Chicago: M.A. Donohue & Co., 1894.
Hartley, Chris J. *Stuart's Tarheels.* Jefferson, NC: McFarland & Co., Inc., 2011.
Jones, John William. *Life and Letters of Robert Edward Lee: Soldier and Man.* New York and Washington: Neale Publishing Company, 1906.
Jones, Reverend J. William, ed. "Brook Church Fight, and Something About the Fifth North Carolina Cavalry." *Southern Historical Society Papers,* Vol. 29, 1901.
Journal of the Sixtieth Annual Convention of the Protestant Episcopal Church in Virginia. Richmond: Elliott & Nye, 1855, 91–92.
Moore, Frank, ed. *The Rebellion Record,* Vol. 11. New York: D. Van Nostrand, 1868.

Mordecai, Emma. Diary, May 1864–May 1865. Virginia Historical Society.

Poindexter, G.W. *An Illustrated History of Bryan Park*. Richmond: Friends of Bryan Park, 2003.

Richmond Dispatch.

Richmond Examiner.

Rodenbough, Theo. F., ed. *The Photographic History of the Civil War*, Vol. 4. New York: Fairfax Press, 1983.

Whitaker, Walter C. *Richard Hooker Wilmer, Second Bishop of Alabama*. Philadelphia: George W. Jacobs & Co., 1907.

CHAPTER 14: FOREIGN ASSISTANCE

Cooke, John Esten. *Mohun, or, The Last Days of Lee and His Paladins*. New York: F.J. Huntington and Co., 1869.

Eaton, Clement. *History of the Southern Confederacy*. New York: Simon and Schuster, 1965.

Gordon, A.C. "Hard Times in the Confederacy." *The Century Illustrated Monthly Magazine* 36 (September 1888): 761–770.

Pickett, La Salle Corbell. *Pickett and His Men*. Atlanta: Foote and Davies Company, 1900.

Richmond Dispatch.

Richmond Enquirer.

CHAPTER 15: RICHMOND'S QUEEN OF HOSPITALITY

"A Confederate Woman's Kind Act Finely Told." *Southern Historical Society Papers*, Vol. 37 (1909): 309–12.

DeLeon, Thomas C. *Belles, Beaux and Brains of the Sixties*. New York: G.W. Dillingham Co., 1909.

Ellet, Elizabeth Fries. *The Queens of American Society*. New York: Charles Scribner & Company, 1867.

Gouverneur, Marian. *As I Remember: Recollections of American Society during the Nineteenth Century*. New York and London: D. Appleton and Company, 1911.

Heidler, David Stephen, Jeanne T. Heidler, David J. Coles. *Encyclopedia of the American Civil War*. New York: W.W. Norton & Company, 2002.

"Lucius Quintus Cincinnatus Lamar." http://mshistorynow.mdah.state.ms.us/articles/173/lucius-quintus-cinncinatus-lamar. Accessed December 12, 2012.

Meade, Robert Douthat. *Judah P. Benjamin: Confederate Statesman*. Baton Rouge: Louisiana State University Press, 2001.

Morgan, James Morris. "The Lost Cause." *The Atlantic Monthly*, Vol. 119. Cambridge: The Riverside Press, 1917.

Patton, John S., ed. *Poems of John R. Thompson*. New York: Charles Scribner's Sons, 1920.

Richmond Dispatch.

Settles, Thomas M. *John Bankhead Magruder: A Military Appraisal*. Baton Rouge: Louisiana State University Press, 2009.

Southern Historical Society Papers. Vol. 16. Richmond: William Ellis Jones, 1888.

Times-Dispatch. "The Westmoreland Club in the History of Richmond from Its Building to the Present Day." June 9, 1912.

Wilson, James Grant. *Thackeray in the United States, 1852–3, 1855–6*. London: Smith, Elder, & Company, 1904.

Woodward, C. Vann, ed. *Mary Chesnut's Civil War*. New Haven: Yale University Press, 1981.

CHAPTER 16: THE DREADED WHIPPING POST

Hening, William Waller. *The Statutes at Large: Being a Collection of All the Laws of Virginia*. Richmond: Samuel Pleasants, Jr., 1810.

Jordan, Ervin L. *Black Confederates and Afro-Yankees in Civil War Virginia*. Charlottesville: University Press of Virginia, 1995.

Richmond Dispatch.

Trammell, Jack. *The Richmond Slave Trade*. Charleston, SC: The History Press, 2012.

"Whipping Post." http://www.vahistorical.org/sva2003/post.htm. Accessed January 5, 2013.

CHAPTER 17: FANFARE AT ROCKETTS WHARF

Furgurson, Ernest B. *Ashes of Glory*. New York: Vintage Books, 1997.

Richmond Dispatch. "Arrival of Confederate Prisoners." May 2, 1864.

————. "Flag of Truce." April 30, 1864.
————. "Returned Confederate Prisoners." May 3, 1864.

CHAPTER 18: BECKMAN'S SALOON DOWN ON MAIN

Lowry, Thomas P., MD. *The Story the Soldiers Wouldn't Tell: Sex in the Civil War.*
  Mechanicsville, PA: Stackpole Books, 1994.
Richmond Dispatch.
Richmond Examiner.

CHAPTER 19: GEORGE ARENTS AND THE LINCOLN CONSPIRACY

Burns, Brian. *Lewis Ginter: Richmond's Gilded Age Icon.* Charleston, SC: The
  History Press, 2011.
Compiled Service Records of Confederate Soldiers who served in organizations
  from the State of Virginia, Reels 15, 213, 364. Library of Virginia.
Confederate Papers Relating to Citizens or Business Firms, 1861–65. National
  Archives, record group 109, roll 0354.
Dabney, Virginius. *Virginia: The New Dominion.* Charlottesville: University
  Press of Virginia, 1983.
Hanchett, William. *The Lincoln Murder Conspiracies.* Urbana: University of
  Illinois Press, 1989.
Hawley, James R. *The Assassination and History of the Conspiracy.* Cincinnati:
  J.R. Hawley & Co., 1865.
Richmond Dispatch.
Richmond Enquirer.
Richmond Examiner.

CHAPTER 20: AVENGING THE "TRAITORESS"

Dowdey, Clifford. *Experiment in Rebellion.* Garden City, NY: Doubleday &
  Company, Inc., 1946.
Furgurson, Ernest B. *Ashes of Glory.* New York: Vintage Books, 197.
Jones, John Beauchamp. *A Rebel War Clerk's Diary at the Confederate States Capital,*
  Vol. 2. Philadelphia: J.B. Lippincott & Co., 1866.

Pollard, Edward Alfred. *Southern History of the War*. New York: C.B. Richardson, 1865.

Richmond Dispatch.

Richmond Enquirer.

Richmond Examiner.

Varon, Elizabeth R. *Southern Lady, Yankee Spy: The True Story of Elizabeth Van Lew, a Union Agent in the Heart of the Confederacy*. New York: Oxford University Press, 2003.

Welsh, Jack D. *Medical Histories of Confederate Generals*. Kent, OH: Kent State University Press.

Winkler, H. Donald. *Stealing Secrets*. Naperville, IL: Cumberland House, 2010.

Chapter 21: Miracle in the Trenches

Richmond Examiner, as referenced in the *Charleston Mercury*. "A Highly Seasoned Joke." June 3, 1864.

Chapter 22: Chester's Campaign

African American National Biography, Vol. 2. New York: Oxford University Press, 2008.

Blackett, R.J.M., ed. *Thomas Morris Chester: Black Civil War Correspondent*. Baton Rouge: Louisiana State University Press, 1989.

Regan, Gerald A. "Man Of Many 'Firsts' Defied Odds." *Times-Dispatch*, March 30, 1995.

INDEX

A

Alexander, George W.
50, 62
Allan, Mary Caroline
115
Arents, George 111
Aylett, P.H. 119, 120

B

Beckman, Henry 109
Benjamin, Judah P. 14,
97
Brook Church 68, 69, 87
Brook Church Fight 87
Brook Hill 46, 70, 75,
88, 89
Brook Road 87, 123
Brook Turnpike 23, 44,
45, 67, 68, 69, 70,
74, 87, 89
Brown's Island 9
Burns, William 115, 119

C

Campbell, John
Archibald 98

Camp Lee 52, 54
Cary, Constance 35
Castle Godwin Prison
78, 108
Castle Thunder Prison
50, 51, 81, 110
Chesnut, Mary 29, 31,
100
Chester, Thomas Morris
125
Confederate coffee 78
Confederate States
Laboratory 9
Cooke, John Esten 93
counterfeiters
Elam, George 84
Richardson, John 84

D

Dahlgren, Colonel Ulric
30, 45
Dahlgren-Kilpatrick
Raid 30, 45
Daniel, John Moncure 29
Davis, Jefferson 27, 29,
30, 31, 33, 45, 55,
60, 85, 99, 106

Davis, Varina 26, 31, 32

E

Emmanuel Church 88
Evacuation of Richmond
101, 110
Exchange Hotel 13, 24

F

faro 13
First African Church 29,
130, 131, 133
fortifications 26, 30, 45,
67
Freedmen's Bureau 64

G

Gilham, Colonel William
H. 58
Ginter, Lewis 111
Godwin, Archibald C.
107
Gordon, Colonel James
Byron 87

H

Hampton, General Wade 97
Hardee, Colonel William J. 55, 57
Hermitage Fairgrounds 54, 55
Hoge, Mrs. Moses D. 117
Hoge, Reverend Moses D. 60, 61, 115, 119, 120

J

Jackson, Thomas J. 57, 63

K

Kilpatrick, General H. Judson 30, 45

L

Lee, Robert E. 57, 73, 89, 132
Les Miserables 92
Letcher, John 55, 57, 89
Lincoln, Abraham 19, 22, 27, 55, 64, 82, 111, 129, 133
Lyons, James 22, 45, 118, 119, 120

M

Mayo, Joseph 10, 13, 16, 102, 127, 133
Mitchell, John, Jr. 26
Mordecai, Emma 65
Mordecai, Rose 65, 67, 68, 73
Mordecai, Rosina. *See* Mordecai, Rose

N

Nero the dog 50, 53

P

Partington, Sallie 48, 53
Peninsula Campaign 20, 35
Polignac, General 28, 61
prisoners 31, 33, 45, 51, 62, 78, 79, 84, 106, 110, 128

R

Randolph, George Wythe 24, 29, 112, 118, 119, 121
Richmond Theatre, The 47, 53
Rocketts Wharf 106, 129, 130
Ryan, Mary 9

S

Semmes, Thomas Jenkins 98
Seven Days' Battles 20, 37, 42, 63
Seward, William H. 27
Sheridan's Raid 68, 89
Shotwell, Hamilton 37, 38
slaves 19, 22, 23, 26, 27, 28, 31, 32, 33, 36, 44, 45, 46, 63, 64, 65, 68, 69, 71, 72, 73, 74, 75, 88, 89, 102, 103, 104, 112, 113, 114, 125
Soulé, Pierre 99
Stanard, Mrs. Robert C. 94

St. Charles Hotel 36, 40
Stearns, Franklin 78
Stewart, John 46, 88
Stuart, J.E.B. 65, 68, 69, 89

T

Taylor, John Oscar 44
Thompson, John R. 98

V

Virginia Cavalier, The 48

W

Walker, Dr. Mary Edwards 79
whipping post 102
Wilmer, Reverend Richard Hooker 88
Winder, General John H. 51, 117
Worsham, Johnny 14

Y

Yellow Tavern 68, 89
Young, John B. 44, 46

ABOUT THE AUTHOR

B rian Burns started his career
in the 1980s as an advertising
art director in North Carolina. He
moved to Richmond in 1987, where
he enjoys a simpler life in writing
and horticulture. His first book was
the 2011 eye-opener *Lewis Ginter:
Richmond's Gilded Age Icon.*